KETO DIET FOR WOMEN
over 50

THE COMPLETE GUIDE FOR REBOOT YOUR METABOLISM STEP-BY-STEP AND QUICKLY BURN FAT. A 40-DAY KETOGENIC MEAL PLAN FOR BEGINNERS.

Amie Cook

Copyright - 2020 -

All rights reserved.

The content contained within this book may not be reproduced, duplicated or transmitted without direct written permission from the author or the publisher.

Under no circumstances will any blame or legal responsibility be held against the publisher, or author, for any damages, reparation, or monetary loss due to the information contained within this book. Either directly or indirectly.

Legal Notice:

This book is copyright protected. This book is only for personal use. You cannot amend, distribute, sell, use, quote or paraphrase any part, or the content within this book, without the consent of the author or publisher.

Disclaimer Notice:

Please note the information contained within this document is for educational and entertainment purposes only. All effort has been executed to present accurate, up to date, and reliable, complete information. No warranties of any kind are declared or implied. Readers acknowledge that the author is not engaging in the rendering of legal, financial, medical or professional advice. The content within this book has been derived from various sources. Please consult a licensed professional before attempting any techniques outlined in this book.

By reading this document, the reader agrees that under no circumstances is the author responsible for any losses, direct or indirect, which are incurred as a result of the use of information contained within this document, including, but not limited to, - errors, omissions, or inaccuracies.

Table of Contents

INTRODUCTION — 4

CHAPTER 1.
THE KETOGENIC DIET — 8

CHAPTER 2.
MORE ABOUT THE KETO DIET — 12

CHAPTER 3.
BENEFITS OF KETO DIET — 16

CHAPTER 4.
INTERMITTENT FASTING — 20

CHAPTER 5.
YOUR INTERMITTENT FASTING AND KETOGENIC DIET LIFESTYLE — 24

CHAPTER 6.
THE KETO & INTERMITTENT FASTING NUTRITION PROGRAM FOR 4 WEEKS — 34

CHAPTER 7.
TIPS ON LOSING WEIGHT ON KETO AFTER 50 — 36

CHAPTER 8.
BREAKFAST RECIPES — 40

CHAPTER 9.
LUNCH RECIPES — 68

CHAPTER 10.
DINNER RECIPES — 94

CHAPTER 11.
SNACKS RECIPES — 122

CHAPTER 12.
BROCHURE ASSOCIATED WITH THE BOOK — 146

CONCLUSION — **188**

Introduction

Getting to the age of 50 means many physical and psychological changes in women such as menopause, hormonal problems, inflammation, irritability, weak muscles and bones, lethargy, and the list goes on. Some women develop diabetes, Alzheimer's, and cardiovascular problems as well.

Why a Normal Keto Diet Is Not Recommended For Women Over 50

With a normal Keto diet, you cut your carbs down to minimum levels, i.e. less than 15 grams. Suddenly severely cutting carbs is bad for you because due to aging your metabolism slows by 25%, and with each passing year, your bones and muscles get weaker and weaker.

We also become more vulnerable to many physiological and psychological diseases, such as cardiovascular disease, obesity, Alzheimer's, or diabetes. Adopting a regular Keto diet plan can result in many side effects, such as:

- Headaches
- Dizziness
- Fatigue
- Brain fog and difficulty focusing
- Lack of motivation and irritability
- Nausea
- Keto flu
- Inflammation

And more!

These side effects cause many women to pull back and lose hope. It's all because you haven't been told before about the likely side effects that you can suffer if you dive headfirst into the Keto diet. However, by consuming the right amount of fats while eating as much as you desire within the range of the specific foods presented in this book, you will get your desired results.

For this, you need a specific Keto diet plan, which will not only benefit you via weight loss but will also help build muscles, stabilizes your blood sugar levels, and maximize your energy levels. And for all this, the Keto diet for women over 50 is a perfect option for you.

HOW THE KETOGENIC DIET CAN AID WITH THE SIGNS AND SYMPTOMS OF AGING AND MENOPAUSE

For aging women, menopause will bring severe changes and challenges, but the ketogenic diet can help you switch gears effortlessly to continue enjoying a healthy and happy life. Menopause can upset hormonal levels in women, which consequently affects brainpower and cognitive abilities. Furthermore, due to less production of estrogens and progesterone, your sex drive declines, and you suffer from sleep issues and mood problems. Let's have a look at how a ketogenic diet will help solve these side effects.

Enhanced Cognitive Functions

Usually, the hormone estrogen ensures the continuous flow of glucose into your brain. But after menopause, the estrogen levels begin to drop dramatically, so does the amount of glucose reaching the bran. As a result, your functional brainpower will start to deteriorate. However, by following the Keto diet for women over 50, the problem of glucose intake is circumvented. This results in enhanced cognitive functions and brain activity.

Hormonal Balance

Usually, women face the main symptoms of menopause due to hormonal imbalances. The Keto diet for women over 50 works by stabilizing these imbalances such as estrogen. This aids in experiencing fewer and bearable menopausal symptoms like hot flashes. The Keto diet also balances blood sugar levels and insulin and helps in controlling insulin sensitivity.

Intensified Sex Drive

The Keto diet surges the absorption of vitamin D, which is essential for enhancing sex drive. Vitamin D ensures stable levels of testosterone and other sex hormones that could become unstable due to low levels of testosterone.

Better Sleep

Glucose disturbs your blood sugar levels dramatically, which in turn leads to poor quality of sleep. Along with other menopausal symptoms, good sleep becomes a huge problem as you age. The Keto diet for women over 50 not only balances blood glucose levels but also stabilizes other hormones like cortisol, melatonin, and serotonin warranting an improved and better sleep.

Reduces inflammation

Menopause can upsurge the inflammation levels by letting potential harmful invaders in our system, which result in uncomfortable and painful symptoms. Keto diet for women over 50 uses healthy anti-inflammatory fats to reduce inflammation and lower pain in your joints and bones.

Fuel your brain

Are you aware that your brain is composed of 60% fat or more? This infers that it needs a larger amount of fat to keep it functioning optimally. In other words, the ketones from the Keto diet serve as the energy source that fuels your brain cells.

Nutrient deficiencies

Aging women tend to have higher deficiencies in essential nutrients such as, iron deficiency, which leads to brain fog and fatigue; Vitamin B12 deficiency, which leads to neurological conditions like dementia; Fats deficiency, that can lead to problems with cognition, skin, vision; and Vitamin D deficiency that not only causes cognitive impairment in older adults and increase the risk of heart disease but also contribute to the risk of developing cancer. On a Keto diet, the high-quality proteins ensure adequate and excellent sources of these important nutrients.

Controlling Blood Sugar

Research has suggested a link between poor blood sugar levels and brain diseases such as Alzheimer's disease, Parkinson's disease, or Dementia. Some factors contributing to Alzheimer's disease may include:

- Enormous intake of carbohydrates, especially from fructose—which is drastically reduced in the ketogenic diet.

- Lack of nutritional fats and good cholesterol — which are copious and healthy in the Keto diet

Keto diet helps control blood sugar and improves nutrition; which in turn not only improves insulin response and resistance but also protects against memory loss, which is often a part of aging.

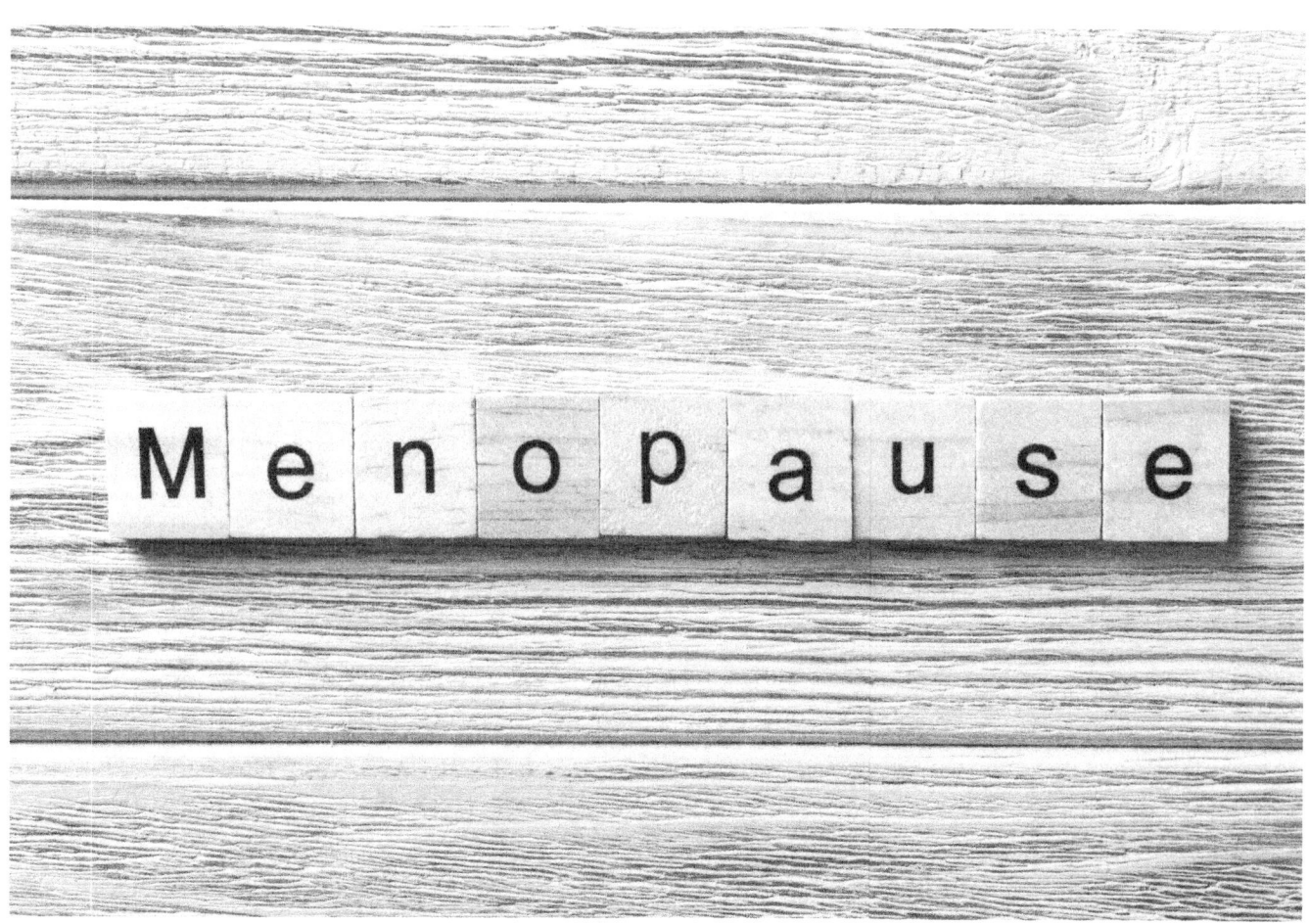

CHAPTER 1.
The Ketogenic Diet

THE CONCEPT OF KETOSIS

WHAT ARE KETONES?
The process begins when you stop eating a lot of carbs over a prolonged period of time. As this occurs, your body will, at some point, burn through the rest of the blood sugar and glycogen stores in your body. Once this happens, your body will begin to search for a different source of fuel. Thanks to the ketogenic diet, this new source of fuel is going to be fat!

When your body discovers the fat to use as fuel, your body will then enter a process that is known as beta-oxidation. This means that your body will begin to use fatty acids for fuel plus the ketones that will begin to form in your liver. While you may feel this is dangerous for the body, it is a safe compound for your body to use as energy.

You see, as your body produces ketone bodies, the excess ketones that your body does happen to produce are going to be eliminated either through your urine or your breath. However, it should be noted that ketones can potentially be an issue for those who have Type 1 or Type 2 Diabetes. These individuals lack insulin, which potentially can build ketones and glucose in the blood system.

TYPES OF KETONES
With that information in mind, it should be noted that there are three different types of ketone bodies. This includes Acetoacetate (Acacia) Beta-hydroxybutyric (BHB) and Acetone. AcAc is created from the breakdown of the fatty acids in your system. This ketone is converted into BHB or can be turned into acetone. BHB is formed from the AcAc, and then the acetone is created as a side product of the AcAc. Typically, acetones are removed from the body through waste and break down rather quickly. These ketones are all in charge of transporting the energy from your liver to the rest of your body.

HOW TO TEST KETONE LEVELS
When you are first starting the ketogenic diet, you will want to choose a method for testing your ketone levels. As you follow the diet more, you will be able to tell if you are in ketosis through the signs and symptoms, but we all have to start somewhere! Luckily for you, there are several different methods to test ketone levels, including urine, breath, and blood. I suggest the blood method, as it is typically the most accurate representation.

On that note, for true beginners, the urine test for ketones may be enough. In the beginning stages, your body is still learning how to use this new fuel. During this time, your body will be filtering quite a bit through your urine, so you will easily be able to tell if your body is producing ketones with a simple test. Over time, your body will adapt, and you will begin to lose fewer ketones through your urine because your body is utilizing them properly.

While following the ketogenic diet, your ketone levels will be anywhere from 0 to 3, and sometimes higher. These ketones are measured in millimoles per liter or mmol/L. You will want to check your general ranges to make sure you are in ketosis and following the diet properly. This is important to know because sometimes, carbs can creep up on you and ruin your process without you even realizing it!

URINE KETONE TESTING
The first method we will discuss is the urine ketone testing method. This method requires you to pee on a urine strip, which will change colors. These can be a good method as they are fairly affordable, and you will be able to find them at most pharmacies. The downfalls for this method are that they aren't always reliable, especially after you've been following the ketogenic diet for a while.

BLOOD KETONE TESTING
This method of testing for ketones is done by a blood glucose meter. This device is a pen that you press into your fingertip to draw a very small blood sample. Once you have your sample, you will apply it to a test strip to monitor your blood ketone levels. This is an excellent method (if you don't mind needles) as it is very accurate. However, it should be noted that this method is a bit expensive. Generally, it will cost you anywhere from $5- $10 per strip.

BREATH KETONE TESTING
Finally, we have the Ketonix breath meter. This device works by measuring the amount of acetone that it detects on your breath. While this is a more affordable option, it isn't always the most reliable. As with urine tests, there are several factors that can change the results, and your body will release fewer ketones into your breath and urine as you learn to use them for fuel.

HOW TO REACH KETOSIS
With a further understanding of ketones and how they work, you may now be wondering how to reach ketosis yourself. While it is a pretty straightforward process, it can seem a bit confusing at first. Below, you will find steps to help you get into ketosis and how to stay there.

RESTRICT CARBOHYDRATES
This may seem obvious, as it the golden rule of the ketogenic diet, but carbohydrates can be tricky. When people first begin this diet, they typically only focus on their net carbs. If you want to lose weight faster, you will want to focus and limit all of your carbohydrates. Generally, you will want to stay below 20g of net carbs and 35g total carbs in a total day.

RESTRICT PROTEIN
As you begin your ketogenic diet, you are going to find that many of the recipes include meat. While this is beneficial for your diet, for the most part, many individuals don't realize that there is such a thing as too much protein. If you consume too much protein in a day, this can lower the levels of ketones in your body. If you are looking to lose weight on the ketogenic diet, you will want to keep your protein levels to .6g and .8g of protein per lean body mass. You can calculate this number using an online calculator.

DRINK WATER

Drinking enough water is going to be vital while following the ketogenic diet. Not only will drinking enough water to keep everything in your body flowing, but it is also going to help you with a number of symptoms that are caused by starting your new diet. It is suggested you drink about a gallon of water per day. This will help regulate your bodily functions and decrease your hunger levels.

THE KETOGENIC DIET AND DISEASES

HEALTH RISKS OF KETOGENIC DIET

Much like with any health decisions you make for yourself, it is important that you compare the risks to the benefits. While it is true that the ketogenic diet does have many incredible benefits, the risks could potentially make this a bad diet for you. Below, you will find some of the more popular risks that come along with practicing the ketogenic diet. While I hope it does work for you, there are many diets out on the market that could be more beneficial to your health.

HYPOTENSION AND SODIUM LOSS

In general, diets that consist of low carbohydrates typically cause the kidneys to excrete sodium at higher levels. This process is known as "natriuresis of starvation" and could potentially be caused by low insulin levels, elevated Glucagon, or increased dopamine excretion. On the ketogenic diet, your carbohydrate levels will be limited, which may limit the sodium intake of your diet. When this happens, your body begins to secrete a hormone known as aldosterone. As this process occurs, the kidneys will excrete potassium and conserve the sodium in your body. When you lose the potassium, this puts you at risk of losing muscle tissue, which could cause muscle cramps and potentially heart arrhythmias.

MINERAL AND VITAMIN DEFICIENCY

Another risk you could be subjecting yourself to on the ketogenic diet could be a deficiency in vital vitamins and minerals. Luckily, this is something that can be easily supplemented into the diet as long as you find a carb-free multivitamin.

This deficiency could potentially lead to easier bone fractures. Individuals on the ketogenic diet generally have lower intakes of vitamin D and calcium. This could potentially lead to lower bone mineral content, leading to easier bone fractures. While this can be supplemented, it is something to keep in mind.

CONSTIPATION

Constipation is a common issue related to the ketogenic diet. This may occur due to the fact that this particular diet is typically low in fiber. You may be able to counterbalance this through a dietary fiber, but it may still be an issue. It is believed that constipation may be due to changes in the intestinal flora as you begin to change your diet. By drinking enough water and supplementing fiber, you may be able to avoid this issue as your body adjusts to the ketogenic diet.

ACIDOSIS

Acidosis is a life-threatening condition that should not be taken lightly. If you are a diabetic patient looking to start the ketogenic diet, this is something that will need to be monitored by a licensed professional. Acidosis occurs in uncontrolled diabetic patients where blood glucose levels become high, and there are high levels of ketones that can become very dangerous. While this is not very common, it has been known to occur when the diet is not done properly. If you experience headaches, vomiting, nausea, or lethargy, you will need to contact a professional immediately.

HYPER KETOSIS

Another major risk that could be presented while following the ketogenic diet is hyper ketosis. In simple terms, this means that there are excessive ketone levels in your system. When this happens, you could experience symptoms, including vomiting, face flushing, a high heart rate, irritability, and rapid panting. In order to stop this, you should have a few tablespoons of orange juice. If this does not help, you should seek immediate medical help.

Now that you have a pretty good base, it is time to dive into starting your journey on the ketogenic diet.

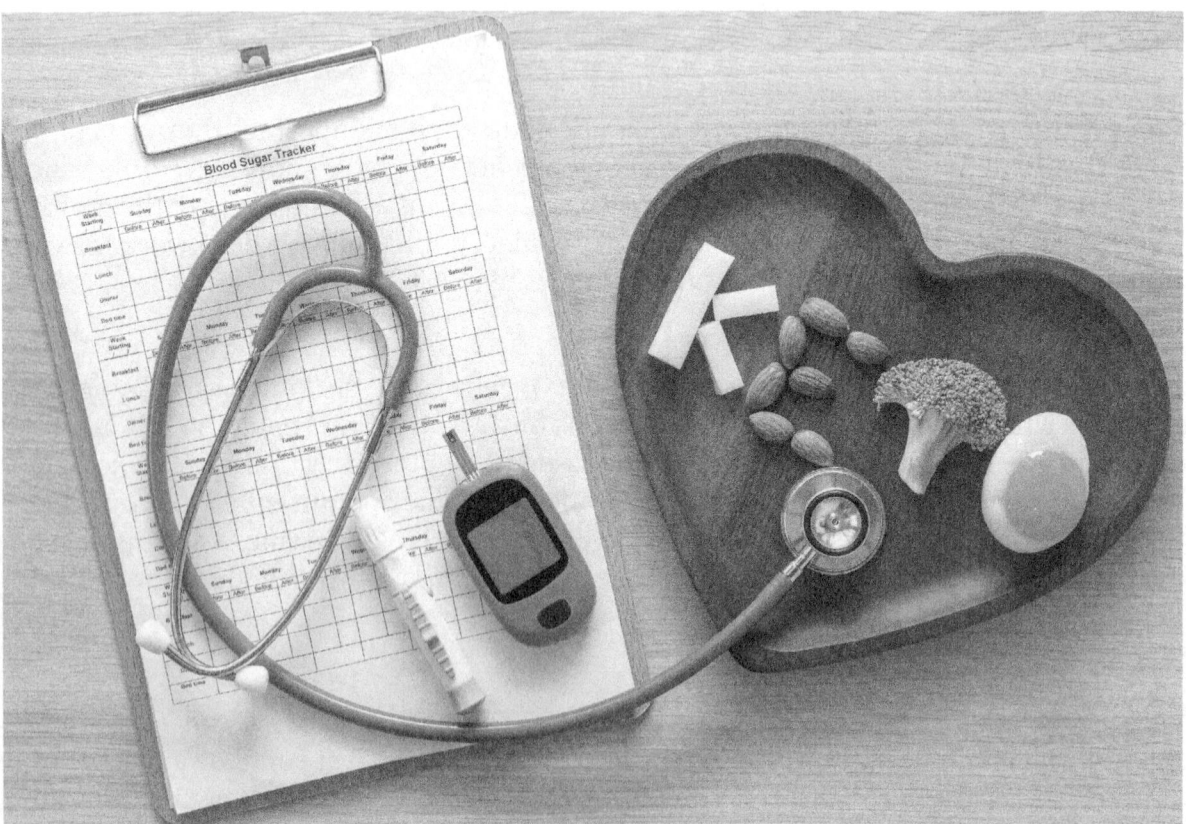

CHAPTER 2.
More about the Keto Diet

If you have reached age fifty, then you should congratulate yourself. You have been through school, teen years, relationships, children, and most especially the changing of your body. You might look at your body and asking it exactly what happened during the last few years. Some things you could not control, like hereditary medical issues and the ravage that time puts on our bodies. Accidents and illnesses are also beyond our control. But you can begin now to understand the changes in your body and make plans to reduce or eliminate as many of the negative changes as you can.

The first thing that will probably happen to you is the onset of menopause. The most notable thing about menopause is that your monthly periods will stop–forever! Menopause is the biggest single change that your body will ever experience besides puberty. Menopause can lead to belly fat, weight gain, and osteoporosis. It is a natural occurrence in the life of every woman, caused by the body making less of the hormones estrogen and progesterone.

Estrogens (there is over one) is the name for the group of sex-related hormones that make women be women. They cause and promote the initial development and further maintenance of female characteristics in the human body. Estrogens gave you breast, hair in the right places, the ability to reproduce, and your monthly cycle. Estrogen is the hormone that does all the long-term work in maintaining femininity. Progesterone has one purpose in the woman's body, and that is to implant the egg in the uterus and keep her pregnant until it is time to deliver the baby.

In women, estrogen is crucial to becoming and remaining womanly. In the ovaries, it stimulates the growth of eggs for reproduction. It causes the vagina to grow to proper adult size. Estrogen promotes the healthy growth of the fallopian tubes and the uterus. And it causes your breasts to grow and to fill with milk when the baby is coming. Estrogen is also responsible for making women store some excess fat around their thighs and hips. This weight storage is nature's way of ensuring that the baby will have nutrition during times of famine.

One form of estrogen dramatically decreases in production after menopause, and this form helps women to regulate the rate of their metabolism and how fast they gain weight. After menopause, women gain more weight in their middle area of the body, in the abdomen. This fat collects around the organs and is known as visceral fat. Besides being unattractive, visceral fat is also dangerous because it's linked to some cancers, heart disease, stroke, and diabetes.

But a lack of estrogen is not the only reason women gain weight after age fifty. Besides a lack of estrogen, the biggest single reason that women over fifty gain weight is lifestyle changes. They are no longer running children to activities; so many women move less after fifty. And sometimes they move less because their joints ached.

MENOPAUSE

There's a lot that the ketogenic diet does to help you reach a healthy and balanced weight and stay there: restore insulin levels of sensitivity, build and maintain muscle mass and lower inflammation. A woman who consumes way too many carbohydrates can jump-start menopause signs. Let's have a look at how a ketogenic diet can aid with the signs and symptoms of this menopause.

WAY # 1 - CONTROLLING INSULIN LEVELS

By going on a ketogenic diet, women with PCOS (polycystic-over-the-air disorder) can help regulate their hormones. Researchers who studied the effect of low-glycemic diets have shown this impact. PCOS triggers insulin sensitivity concerns, to be helped by insulin-reducing properties of low-glycemic carbohydrates.

WAY # 2 - YOU'LL HAVE MORE ENERGY

Our bodies will experience widely known energy dips if we fuel them with mainly sugar and carbohydrates. Especially if you take in quick and refined sugars (think about carrot cake, cupcakes, crackers, bread, candy, etc.). Changes in blood glucose can stop by receiving a steady amount of sugar. High blood glucose makes the body send insulin to the pancreas, which then takes care of how muscular tissue and fat cells absorb sugar.

The reaction to the consumption of carbs is a powerful release of insulin to make sure that the body can properly manage the transport of the extra sugar. With blood sugar levels down, the body will signal that it requires more sugar. This means you'll experience many energy lows and highs in one day. This produces a reduced energy level.

WAY # 3 - FAT BURNING

Menopause can trigger the metabolic process to change and reduce. One of the most common complaints of menopause is an increase in body weight and abdominal fat. A lower level of estrogen typically causes weight gain. A diet with little or no carbohydrates is very efficient for decreasing body fat. Ketosis reduces appetite by controlling the production of the 'cravings hormonal agent' called ghrelin. You are less hungry while in ketosis.

WAY # 4 - REDUCTION IN HOT FLASHES

Nobody totally understands hot flashes and why they take place. Hormonal changes that impact the hypothalamus; most likely have something to do with this. The hypothalamus manages the body's temperature level. Changes in hormonal agents can also disrupt this thermostat. This ends up being more sensitive to modifications in body temperature levels.

Ketone, in which its production stimulates throughout a ketogenic diet, creates a very potent source of energy for the mind. Scientists have shown that ketones act to help the hypothalamus. The body will manage its own temperature level better. The presence of ketones works to make your body's thermostat better.

WAY # 5 - EXCELLENT NIGHT'S REST

Thanks to a much steadier blood sugar level, you will improve rest while on a ketogenic diet. With even more balanced hormones and much less warm flashes, you will sleep better. Reduced stress and enhanced well-being are 2 of the benefits of better sleep.

THE KETOGENIC DIET AND WEIGHT LOSS

Losing weight: for most people, this is the foremost benefit of switching to Keto! Their previous diet method may have stalled for them or they were noticing weight creeping back on. With Keto, studies have shown that people have been able to follow this diet and relay fewer hunger pangs and suppressed appetite while losing weight at the same time! You are minimizing your carbohydrate intake, which means fewer blood sugar spikes. Often, those fluctuations in blood sugar levels make you feel more hungry and prone to snacking in between meals. Instead, by guiding the body towards ketosis, you are eating a more fulfilling diet of fat and protein and harnessing energy from ketone molecules instead of glucose. Studies show that low-carb diets are very effective in reducing visceral fat (the fat you commonly see around the abdomen that increases as you become obese). This reduces your risk of obesity and improves your health in the long run.

HORMONE BALANCE

With a more thorough understanding of how the ketogenic diet can help balance your hormones, it is time to learn how! By embracing the ketogenic life and applying these lessons to your everyday life, you will enjoy this diet in no time. Remember that while it will take some extra effort at first, it will be thoroughly worth it. The first thing you will want to do is focus on your diet! One of the most beneficial steps you can take is starting eating foods rich in probiotics. By doing this, you will keep your gut bacteria in check. Also, plan to eat more protein for about three days before your period, to help keep your hormones in check.

Another way you can help your hormone balance is to eat foods rich in calcium. Foods such as almonds, salmon, celery, sesame, and poppy can help with symptoms that are associated with mood swings. If you ever have questions, you can always test your hormone levels to make sure they are in check. The ones you will want to pay special attention to include cortisol, progesterone, estrogen, and SBHG. While this isn't diet-related, managing your stress levels is a vital part of balancing your hormones. Remember that stress had a major effect on your hormones, so you need to address the issue at hand. To help combat stress, remember to move your body, sleep well, and spend time with your loved ones.

Finally, you will want to test your pH levels. As we age, maintaining the alkalinity within your diet will be key. Alkalinity has a direct effect on your vitamin absorption, lowers inflammation, improved bone density, and helps you maintain a healthy weight. Luckily on the ketogenic diet, you will balance this in your diet.

ALKALINE KETOGENIC DIET

You are already well aware of what the ketogenic diet is, but what is an alkaline diet? We base this dieting around eating acidic foods that alter your pH balance. As you eat, your metabolism breaks down the food into metabolic waste through chemical reactions. The metabolic waste is acidic (pH under 7.0), neutral (pH of 7.0), or is alkaline (pH over 7.0). According to the alkaline diet, the pH of your metabolic waste influences your body's acidity. When your body is too acidic, this leads to health issues such as heart disease, cancer, diabetes, hypertension, and osteoporosis. To improve the acidity of your body, create an alkaline state in your body through diet.

When you create an alkaline environment in your body through the ketogenic diet, you will experience incredible benefits such as lowering inflammation within the body, balancing your hormones, and slow down the aging process. An alkaline diet can also help support your overall health by reducing the symptoms often in association with infertility, menopause, and PMS.

Your body is naturally alkaline. Depending on what you eat can heighten or lower your pH balance. Much like with testing ketones, you can test your pH balance through a urine testing kit. In an ideal world, you want to strive for a pH between 7.0 and 7.5. The question is, how?

The answer you are looking for is the ketogenic diet. When you combine an alkaline diet with a low-carb diet, you are lowering the number of toxic substances you are sticking in your body and providing it with more nutrients through your new diet.

To further your process, fasting is another way to keep yourself healthy and allows your body the time to take a break from the function of digesting. By doing this, your body has time to repair other parts of you and can send its energy toward helping the cells rather than digesting your dinner!

With all of this in mind, note that the ketogenic diet, while beneficial, may not completely solve your issues. There are other problems that can cause hormonal issues such as hypo/hyperthyroidism, over-training, stress, not eating enough, and other pre-existing hormonal balances. If you continue to struggle with your hormones, get checked out by a professional. As earlier said, there are benefits to the ketogenic diet, but it will not cure you by magic. That said, if it doesn't help your hormonal balance that does not mean you will not experience other enjoyment from your new diet; stick with it!

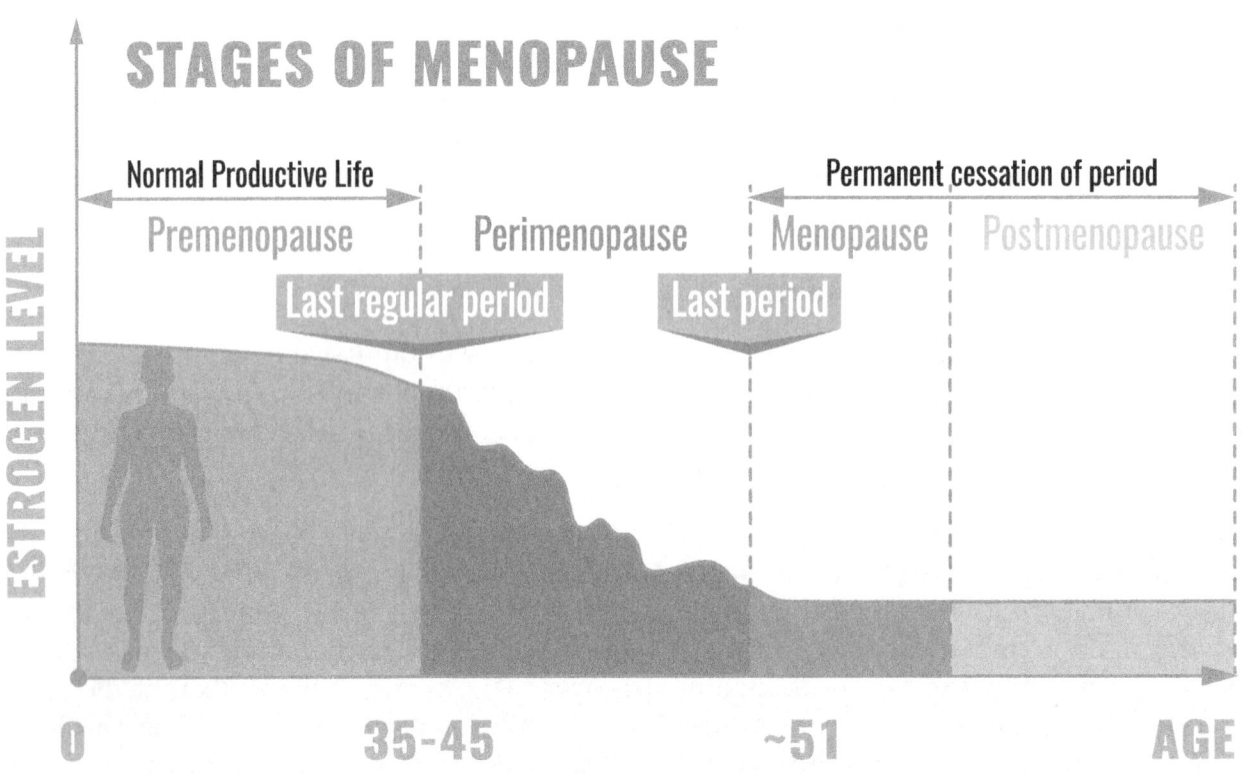

CHAPTER 3.
Benefits of Keto Diet

The Keto diet has become so popular in recent years because of the success people have noticed. Not only have they managed to lose weight, but scientific studies show that the Keto diet can help you improve your health in many others. As when starting any new diet or exercise routine, there may seem to be some disadvantages so we will go over those for the Keto diet as well. But most people agree that the benefits outweigh the adjustment period!

DECREASES THE RISK OF TYPE 2 DIABETES

The problem with carbohydrates is how unstable they make blood sugar levels. This can be very dangerous for people who have diabetes or are considered pre-diabetic due to unstable blood sugar levels or family history. Keto is a great option because of the minimal intake of carbohydrates it requires. Instead, you are harnessing the majority of your calories from fat or protein, which will not cause blood sugar spikes and ultimately put less pressure on the pancreas to secrete insulin. Many studies have found that diabetes patients who followed the Keto diet lost more weight and ultimately reduced their fasting glucose levels. This is great news for patients who have unstable blood sugar levels or are hoping to avoid or reduce their diabetes medication intake.

IMPROVE CARDIOVASCULAR RISK SYMPTOMS TO OVERALL LOWER YOUR CHANCES OF HAVING HEART DISEASE.

Most people assume that following Keto that is so high in fat content has to increase your risk of coronary heart disease or heart attack. But the research proves otherwise! Research shows that switching to Keto can lower your blood pressure, increase your HDL good cholesterol, and reduce your triglyceride fatty acid levels. That's because the fats you are consuming on Keto are healthy and high-quality fats so they tend to reverse many unhealthy symptoms of heart disease. They boost your "good" HDL cholesterol numbers and decrease your "bad" LDL cholesterol numbers. It also decreases the level of triglyceride fatty acids in the bloodstream. A high level of these can lead to stroke, heart attack, or premature death. And what are the high levels of fatty acids linked to? High consumption of carbohydrates. With the Keto diet, you are drastically cutting your intake of carbohydrates to improve fatty acid levels and improve other risk factors. A 2018 study on the Keto diet found that it can improve as many as 22 out of 26 risk factors for cardiovascular heart disease! These factors can be very important to some people, especially those who have a history of heart disease in their family.

INCREASES THE BODY'S ENERGY LEVELS.
We compared briefly the difference between the glucose molecules synthesized from a high carbohydrate intake versus ketones produced on the Keto diet. Ketones are made by the liver and use fat molecules you already have stored. This makes them much more energy-rich and a lasting source of fuel compared to glucose, a simple sugar molecule. These ketones can give you a burst of energy physically as well as mentally allow you to have greater focus, clarity, and attention to detail.

DECREASES INFLAMMATION IN THE BODY
Inflammation on its own is a natural response by the body's immune system, but when it becomes uncontrollable, it can lead to an array of health problems, some severe, some minor. The many health concerns include acne, autoimmune conditions, arthritis, psoriasis, irritable bowel syndrome, and even acne and eczema. Often, removing sugars and carbohydrates from your diet can help patients of these diseases avoid flare-ups - and the good news is Keto does just that! A 2008 research study found that Keto decreased a blood marker linked to high inflammation in the body by nearly 40%. This is great news for people who may suffer from inflammatory disease and are willing to change their diet to hopefully see improvement.

INCREASES YOUR MENTAL FUNCTIONING LEVEL
As we explained earlier, energy-rich ketones can boost the body's physical and mental levels of alertness. Research has shown that Keto is a much better energy source for the brain than simple sugar glucose molecules are. With nearly 75% of your diet coming from healthy fats, the brain's neural cells and mitochondria have a better source of energy to be able to function at the highest level. Some studies have tested patients on the Keto diet and found they had higher cognitive functioning, better memory recall, and were less susceptible to memory loss. The Keto diet can even decrease the occurrence of migraines, which can be very detrimental to patients.

DECREASES RISK OF DISEASES LIKE ALZHEIMER'S, PARKINSON'S, AND EPILEPSY.
The Keto diet was actually created in the 1920s as a way to combat epilepsy in children. From there, research has found that Keto can improve your cognitive functioning level and protect brain cells from injury or damage. This is very good to reduce the risk of neurodegenerative disease, which begins in the brain due to neural cells mutating and functioning with damaged parts or lower than peak optimal functioning. Studies have found that following Keto can improve the mental functioning of patients who suffer from diseases like Alzheimer's or Parkinson's. These neurodegenerative diseases sadly have no cure, but the Keto diet could improve symptoms as they progress. Researchers believe that is due to cutting out carbs from your diet, which reduces the occurrence of blood sugar spikes that the body's neural cells have to continually adjust to.

CAN REGULATE HORMONES IN WOMEN WHO HAVE PCOS AND PMS
Women who have PCOS (polycystic ovary syndrome) suffer from infertility, which can be very heartbreaking for young couples trying to start a family. There is no cure for this condition, but it is believed that it is related to many similar diabetic symptoms like obesity and high insulin levels. This causes the body to produce more sex hormones, which can lead to infertility. The Keto diet has become a popular method to try and regulate insulin and hormone levels and could increase a woman's chances of getting pregnant.

DISADVANTAGES

Your body will have an adjustment period. It depends from person to person on how many days that will be, but when you start any new diet or exercise routine, your body has to adjust to the new normal. With the Keto diet, you are drastically cutting your carbohydrates intake, so the body has to adjust to that. You may feel slow, weak, fatigued, and like you are not thinking as quick or fast as you used to. It just means your body is adjusting to Keto and once this adjustment period is done, you will see the weight loss results you anticipated.

If you are an athlete, you may need more carbohydrates. If you still want to try Keto as an athlete, you must talk to your nutritionist or trainer to see how the diet can be tweaked for you. Most athletes require a greater intake of carbs than the Keto diet requires, which means they may have to up their intake in order to assure they have the energy for their training sessions. High endurance sports (like rugby or soccer) and heavy weightlifting do require a greater intake of carbohydrates. If you're an athlete wanting to follow Keto and gain the health benefits, it's important you first talk to your trainer before making any changes to your diet.

You have to carefully count your daily macros! For beginners, this can be tough, and even people already on Keto can become lazy about this. People are often used to eating what they want without worrying about just how many grams of protein or carbs it contains. With Keto, you have to be meticulous about counting your intake to ensure you are maintaining the necessary Keto breakdown (75% fat, 20% protein, ~5% carbs). The closer you stick to this, the better results you will see regarding weight loss and other health benefits. If your weight loss has stalled or you're not feeling as energetic as you hoped, it could be because your macros are off. Find a free calorie counting app that and be sure you look at the ingredients of everything you're eating and cooking.

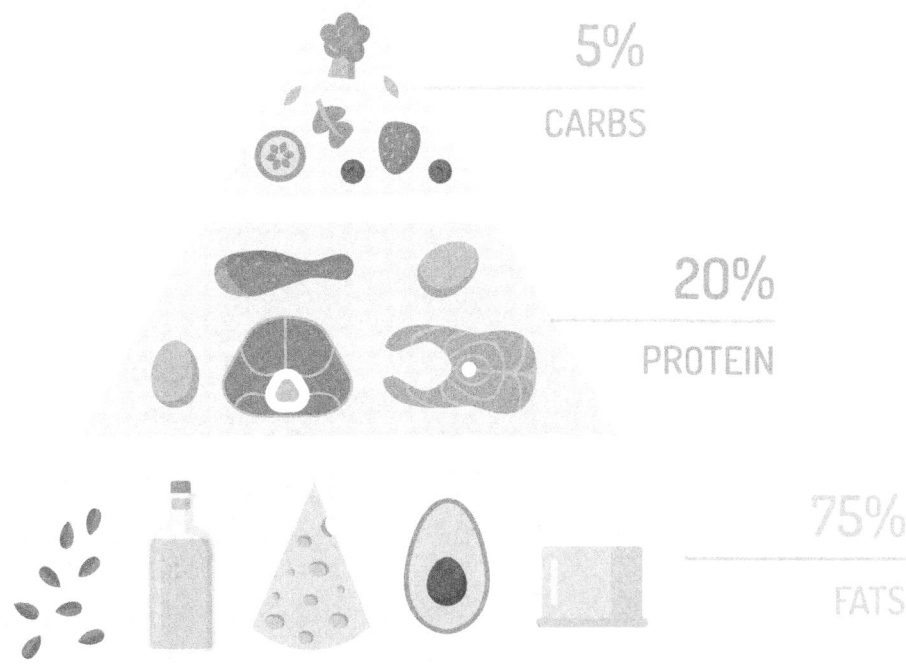

CHAPTER 4.
Intermittent Fasting

WHAT IS INTERMITTENT FASTING?

Fasting is basically defined as a deliberate abstention from eating. It is the deliberate action of depriving the body of food and calories for more than six hours. Intermittent fasting is one of the forms of fasting, in which the fast is carried out in a cyclic manner with the goal of cutting down the overall caloric intake in a day. To most people, it may seem unhealthy and damaging to health, but scientific studies and research have proven that fasting can produce positive results for both the human mind and body. It teaches discipline and fights against unhealthy eating habits. It is a wide umbrella term that is used to define all forms of fasting. This dietary approach does not restrict the intake of specific food items; rather, it works by reducing the overall food intake, leaving enough space to meet the essential body needs. Therefore, it is proven to be far more effective and much easier in implementation, given that the dieter completely understands the nature and science of intermittent fasting.

TYPES OF INTERMITTENT FASTING

Intermittent fasting is not one fixed formula for all; rather, it is a flexible regime of calorie restriction. The modified intermittent fasting program is the result of several approaches combined under one head, giving its users a flexible path to adapt according to their particular age, gender, and rates of metabolism. Research on fasting patterns has shown that certain fasting methods are healthier and more beneficial than others. The following are the different methods of intermittent fasting that can be used by women over the age of 50.

1. THE CRESCENDO METHOD

Having recently surfaced, this method of intermittent fasting was readily adopted by people of all ages and gender. The method has also been proven effective for women over 50, as it sets a practical fasting limit and provides a weekly schedule without limiting the caloric intake. The crescendo method suggests about 12 to 16 hours of fasting but for only two or three days a week. That means if a woman chooses a 12-hour limit for the fast, then she can fast for three days in a week and for about two days if the fasting limit is around 16 hours. It is said that these days must be non-consecutive; for example, Friday, Sunday, and Tuesday. The method brings much-needed ease and convenience to all women and does not cause extreme deprivation, weakness, or hunger pangs. Moreover, the non-consecutive approach provides essential relief to the body and gives constant food breaks.

2. THE 5:2 METHOD

Once you have decided the number of hours, you can select the method of intermittent fasting according to the days. The 5:2 methods prescribe the number of days to fast in a week. In this method, a person can fast for two days a week and normally eat during the other five days. The modified 5:2 method also prescribes a caloric limit for two of its fasting days. For women, the caloric intake should not be more than 500 calories on the day of the fast, whereas there is no such restriction for the rest of the five days of the week. This low caloric intake can be easily maintained by having healthy organic food before and after the fast. The two fasting days can be any two days of the week, given that they are non-consecutive. The selection of the days depends on personal preference. For instance, working women can choose to fast on Friday and on the weekend so as not to disrupt their work routine.

3. THE ALTERNATE DAY FASTING

This method is usually called the "Up-Day, Down-Day Fasting" method, which means that a person needs to fast on the alternating days of the week. It involves one day of fasting, and the next day is specified for eating. When and how to initiate the fast and for how many hours, it depends on personal preference. But the day of fasting must restrict the caloric intake down to 500 calories for women. Ladies! You can maintain this restriction by completely avoiding solid food during the fast while taking low caloric food before and after the fast.

4. HALF-DAY OR 12-HOUR FASTING METHOD

The 12 hours of fast in a day is one of the most balanced approaches and suits people of all body types and work routines. A person can decide himself about the time frame of this 12-hour fast. For example, it can start at 7 pm in the evening and continue till 7 am in the morning. In this way, most of the fasting period is spent during sleep. You can have a meal in the evening then break the fast in the morning with a healthy and rich breakfast. This 12-hour regime is quite suitable for all beginners. If a person chooses this 12-hour program, then it is recommended to fast every other day or on alternate days of the week to achieve weight loss goals and other health benefits.

5. THE 16:8 METHOD

The 16:8 methods, also called the lean gain method, shows the ratio of the fasting hours to the hours of the FED state. In this method, a person should fast for 16 hours a day, which gives him an 8-hour period to eat. It depends on the person how many meals to add to this eating period. There can be two or three meals during this time. Such meals need to be rich in content so that they could meet the nutritional needs in a short duration. The 16 hours of fasting seems too difficult to follow, and it is usually not suggested to beginners and those having diabetes. But it is suitable for those who can't fast every other day or who need to quickly achieve their weight loss. Healthy women can surely opt for this method, but most women are suggested to reduce the fasting duration to 15 to 14 hours then gradually move towards the 16 hours method.

6. THE 14/10 METHOD

Since not every woman can comfortably follow the 16:8 intermittent fasting method due to her health concerns, there is yet another method to go for. In this routine, a woman can fast for 14 hours and eat for 10 hours in a day. This window is enough to satisfy all the energy and caloric needs of the body. To implement this method with ease, start the fast at around even in the evening then break the fast at nine in the morning. This routine is best suited for working women, who can then easily eat food during their work hours.

7. 24 HOURS OR EAT STOP EAT METHOD

Some people may describe it as the toughest of all the methods of intermittent fasting, whereas others consider it to be more convenient than fasting every other day. The 24-hour fast seems like a tough job for those who can't endure hunger pangs for too long. It is also hazardous for women suffering from certain nutritional deficiencies, cancer, and diabetes, as it may lead to extremely low levels of glucose in the blood. The method is, however, suitable for people with greater stamina and strength. It is an expert-level fasting method, so a person can switch to this method after a few months of fasting through other methods. Though it is a more rigorous technique, it does save a person from a regular fast. During those 24 hours, you can consume water and zero caloric beverages while avoiding solid food. The fast can extend from one dinner to another, or lunch to lunch or breakfast to breakfast.

In a 24-hour fast, a person must avoid extraneous exercises or intense physical activity to keep the energy levels maintained throughout the fast.

INTERMITTENT FASTING ON KETO DIET

Intermittent fasting works best when it is paired with a healthy dietary approach. The ketogenic diet, in this regard, rightly complements intermittent fasting as it provides a good amount of lasting energy to the dieter during the fast. Carbs are the immediate source of energy that is quickly metabolized and used, whereas fats provide energy through a gradual breakdown, which keeps the dieter energized during the fast. Thus, experts recommend a high fat and a low-carb diet to harness the true benefits of intermittent fasting.

1. FOLLOW THE CALORIC LIMIT

Every method of intermittent fasting prescribes a certain caloric limit, which must be taken into consideration while planning a ketogenic meal for a fasting day. Reduce the number of calories without compromising on the balanced proportion of both the micro and macronutrients. Take more smoothies and zero caloric juices to keep the caloric intake in check. During the non-fasting days of the week, the meal plan must follow through a balanced approach, which must include small and frequent meals throughout the day.

2. DEPEND MORE ON FATS

The meal before the fast holds more important! It should be rich with fats so that the body will receive a constant supply of energy throughout the day. Use different sources of fats in one meal to keep a variety of flavors.

3. SLOWLY BREAK THE FAST

Eating everything at once at the time of breaking the fast is going to reverse the effects of fasting. Even when you are on a ketogenic diet, you must break the fast with a small meal like a smoothie, then take a break and have another small meal. In this way, the excess fats will not be stored in the body.

4. FOCUS ON HYDRATION

Intermittent fasting does not restrict a person from having zero caloric fluids and water. Since ketogenic lifestyle demands more hydration, a person must constantly consume water during the fast and after it to keep the body hydrated all the time. Muscle and body fatigue can be avoided with active hydration.

5. MAKE SMART CHOICES

Since fasting reduces the overall meal consumption during a day or a week, it requires better and healthy food to meet the nutritional needs of the body. A person does not need fillers on this diet; he must consume rich food with a variety of protein sources like meat and seafood along with nuts, oils, and vegetables. Make smarter choices and try to add multiple low-carb ingredients in a single platter to have all the essential nutrients in every meal.

CHAPTER 5.
Your Intermittent Fasting and Ketogenic Diet Lifestyle

WHAT TO EAT

1. FATS AND OILS

Fats play a big role when it comes to weight loss with one of these roles is making foods that you consume better for you. How is that? Well, for starters, some nutrients and vitamins like vitamins A, D, E, and K are fat-soluble. This essentially means that you need some fat for your body to use them efficiently. In other words, if you don't take fats, your body won't be able to utilize them since they will be unavailable for the cells (the fat helps in facilitating the absorption of these vitamins). As you are already aware, in case the body cannot absorb nutrients as required, you develop nutrient deficiencies, which could come with such complications as blood clots, muscle pains, brittle bones, and blindness among others.

More precisely, the vitamins mentioned above are useful in sustainable energy production, muscle health and focus; all of which facilitate weight loss. For instance, vitamin E is an antioxidant while vitamin D may help the body utilize fat that occurs in the abdominal region.

In the Ketogenic diet, fat works as an alternative source of energy and indeed helps trigger the ketosis process or breakdown of fats into energy. To facilitate weight loss, you should take fats and oils rich in omega 3 fatty oils, from sources like salmon, tuna, and trout. You are required to include both saturated and mono-saturated fats like avocados, egg yolks, butter, macadamia nuts, and coconut oils as these are healthier.

Chicken fat

Butter

Peanut butter

Avocado

Coconut oil

None hydrogenated lard

Olive oil

2. PROTEINS

Protein forms a significant part of the Keto diet plan, as it helps in the synthesis and monitoring of hormones in the bloodstream. Hormones control bodily functions.

In the Keto diet, good sources of protein include eggs, fish, and meat. While any meat is protein-rich, a few rules should be followed when choosing your source of meat. The rule of thumb is to go for organic and grass feed meat in place of that grain-fed meat, as corn fed to domestic animals is genetically modified, rich in hormones and antibiotics. For this reason, go for all-natural beef, pork or mutton as well as organic and free-range turkey or chicken.

When it comes to bacon, go for nitrate-free bacon and that without other additives; and wild-caught fish, as opposed to the farm, reared.

Here is a complete list of protein foods:

Lean Meats

Beef

Chicken

Turkey

Pork

Lamb

Game meat

Pork

Bacon

Seafood and Fish

Haddock

Trout

Shrimp

Salmon

Catfish

Tuna

Mackerel

Codfish

Poultry

Turkey: whole, breast, leg portions, or ground

Quail

Pre-cooked Rotisserie Chicken

Pre-cooked chicken strips

Pheasant

Goose

Duck

Deli meats: Turkey, Chicken, no nitrates

Cornish Hens

Chicken, whole and whole cut-up

Chicken Tenders

Canned Chicken

Chicken pieces: breasts, wings, thighs, legs

Pork

Sausages

Pork Tenderloin

Pork Steaks

Pork Roasts

Pork Chops

Italian Sausage

Ham

Ground Pork

Deli – Ham

Bacon

3. VEGGIES

Veggies such as kales, broccoli, and spinach are sources of vitamins and minerals; and they are low-carb and satiating. Try the following veggies and other dark leafy greens such as those listed here:

Onions

Tomatoes

Garlic

Asparagus

Collard greens

Broccoli

Parsley

Peppers

Carrots

Cauliflower

Cabbage

Spinach

Turnips

Kales

4. LOW CARB FRUITS
While fruits are very nutritious and satiating, it is advisable to eat them in moderation particularly if trying to lose weight. This is because fruits contain fructose, a type of sugar that could easily get you out of ketosis and make you gain weight. Therefore, don't over-indulge in fruits; rather, limit your intake to around 1-2 fruit servings daily.

Likewise, avoid starchy fruits and fruit juices, as these have very high concentrations of carbs and sugars. When eaten in moderation, the following fruits are healthy and nutritious:

Oranges

Apples

Avocadoes

Pears

Berries (all types)

Pineapples

Papaya

5. NUTS AND SEEDS
For nuts and seeds, these are rich in healthy and satiating omega-3 fatty acids but should be moderated too as they tend to be high in carbs. Try eating these foods as snacks occasionally:

Walnuts

Macadamia nuts

Hazelnuts

Pumpkin seeds

Sunflower seeds

Flaxseed

Almonds

6. Dairy

While it may come as a great surprise, you should not drink or use milk in its natural form. This is because cow's milk contains allergens such as lactose (a form of sugar) that some dieters are intolerant to. But for cheese, yogurt and other fermented dairy products, these are Ketogenic friendly and should form a large part of your diet. However, if you cannot keep off milk, try almond or coconut milk as these are suitable for blending other ingredients and actually improve the milk flavor. Try the following dairy alternatives:

Cheese

Butter

Ricotta cheese

Full Fat Cheese, use sparingly

Almond Milk

Greek or plain yogurt

Full Fat Cottage Cheese

Butter

Cream, or whipped cream

Coconut Milk

7. SPICES
You should be very careful about the spices you use, as some have high concentrations of carbohydrates. Even the common table salt is usually mixed with powdered dextrose; you might want to consider using sea salt. Here is a list of spices that are good for low carb diets.

Sea salt

Black pepper

Cinnamon

Chili powder

Turmeric

Parsley

Rosemary

Sage

WHAT TO AVOID
1. ALL GRAINS
These include rice, wheat, barley, and oats; along with products that come from them such as crackers, bagels, cereal, pasta, granola bars, and bread. Simply avoid every food material that has grain in it, whether whole-grain, processed grains, or whatever kind of grains you can come across. Instead, try almond or coconut flour, as these have low carb content, have high fiber levels, and are rich in proteins.

2. STARCHY VEGGIES
Leafy dark leafy greens are Keto friendly but avoid their starchy variety. These include popcorn, tortillas, corn chips, potatoes chips, corn, and white potatoes.

3. BEANS OR LEGUMES

The ketogenic diet limits intake of carbs to at most 50 grams daily so you must avoid all high carb foods such as beans and legumes for that matter. To further control your carb intake, you shouldn't eat spaghetti squash, pumpkins, acorn, butternut squash, summer squash, and sweet potatoes.

4. SUGARY FOODS AND DRINKS

High carb foods and drinks include candies, cookies, sport drinks, cakes, honey, soda, syrup, and jam or jelly. These may spike blood sugar, disrupt insulin function, and can trigger unnecessary cravings a few hours after eating. Also avoid fruit juices at all costs, as they tend to have too much sugar and thus cannot be Keto friendly.

5. VEGETABLE OILS

Although the Ketogenic diet is high in fat, this doesn't mean you can eat all fats. Avoid vegetable oils such as sunflower oil, corn oil, safflower, and other hydrogenated oils. These are comprised of Tran's fats, which are linked to cardiovascular problems.

6. HIGH CARB DRINKS

Here are a number of drinks that you should stay away from:

BEERS

Beers are a product of grain, which has high carb content. Alcohol also slows fat burning. If you have to drink, take low carb beers like vodka, tequila, whiskey, gin, rum, cognac, and brandy.

NON-DIET SODAS

Sweetened soda pops contain large amounts of fructose; a type of carbohydrate found in most fruits. For example, corn syrup has lots of carbs that you should avoid.

HOW TO GET STARTED

A typical breakdown of a Keto diet would be Fat: 70%, Carbs: 5%, and Protein: 25%.

Your daily net carbs intake should be 20-30 grams to stay in Ketosis.

Limit your fruit consumption to avocados, berries, and coconut.

Drink more water. You need to drink 2-3 liters of water daily.

Say no to carb dressings, spreads, sweeteners, or high carb nuts.

Make sure you are eating no carbs at all, and also keep track of your meal intake.

Eat fatty breakfast and eat one fat in each meal.

Stock your pantry with healthy foods, i.e., meat, eggs, starchy vegetables, avocados, saturated fats, like, coconut oil, ghee, olive oil, sesame oil, flaxseed oil.

Eat raw dairy, but if you are allergic, avoid it.

Soak and dehydrate nuts before you eat them.

Drink Bone Broth every day.

Increase your electrolytes (sodium, magnesium, and potassium) intake to keep yourself safe from Keto flu.

Plan and track your diet carefully.

SET YOUR GOAL

The saying remains true — you will realize that what you put into your body is going to dictate how you feel. While on the Keto diet, you are building up energy stores for your body to utilize. This means that you should be feeling a necessary boost in your energy levels and the ability to get through each moment of each day without struggling. You can say goodbye to the sluggish feeling that often accompanies other diet plans. When you are on Keto, you should only be experiencing the benefits of additional energy and unlimited potential. Your diet isn't going to always feel like a diet. After some time, you will realize that you actually enjoy eating a Keto menu very much. Because your body is going to be switching the way it metabolizes, it will also be switching what it craves. Don't be surprised if you end up craving fats and proteins as you progress on the Keto diet — this is what your body will eventually want.

SHOPPING LIST

Following are the foods that are emphasized on a Keto diet:

- Healthy, fatty fish such as tuna, salmon, etc.
- Healthy oils such as avocado oil, coconut oil, olive oil, etc.
- All types of full-fat cheese and full-fat cream cheese, sour cream, crème Fraiche.
- Unsweetened almond/coconut milk, or other nut milk
- Eggs
- Butter, total fat
- Avocados
- Walnuts, almonds, cashews, and other nuts
- Chia seed and flaxseed
- Olives
- Bacon
- Unsweetened beverages
- Heavy cream
- Healthy low carb, non-starchy veggies such as leek, fennel, spinach, kale, broccoli, tomatoes, other greens, etc.
- All types of berries but in small quantities
- Herbs and most spices

FOOD CONVERSION TABLE APPENDIX
Conversion Table from the US to Europe Measurements

U.S Weight Measure
- 1/2 ounce
- 1 ounce
- 2 ounces
- 3 ounces
- 1/4 pound (4 ounces)
- 1/2 pound (8 ounces)
- 3/4 pound (12 ounces)
- 1 pound (16 ounces)
- 2.2 pounds (35.25 ounces)

Metric Equivalent
- 14 grams
- 28 grams
- 57 grams
- 85 grams
- 113 grams
- 227 grams
- 340 grams
- 454 grams
- 1 kilogram

Length
- 1/8 inch
- 1/4 inch
- 1/2 inch
- 1 inch
- 2 inches
- 4 inches
- 5 inches
- 6 inches
- 12 inches (1 foot)

Metric Equivalent
- 3 millimeters
- 6 millimeters
- 11/4 centimeters
- 21/2 centimeters
- 5 centimeters
- 10 centimeters
- 13 centimeters
- 15-1/4 centimeters
- 30 centimeters

Oven Temperature Conversions

Degrees Fahrenheit

- 200°F
- 225°F
- 250°F
- 275°F
- 300°F
- 325°F
- 350°F
- 375°F
- 400°F
- 425°F
- 450°F
- 475°F
- 600°F

Degrees Celsius

- 95°C
- 110°C
- 120°C
- 135°C
- 150°C
- 160°C
- 180°C
- 190°C
- 200°C
- 220°C
- 230°C
- 245°C
- 316°C

CHAPTER 6.
The Keto & Intermittent Fasting Nutrition Program for 4 Weeks

Week 1

Day	Breakfast	Lunch	Dinner	Snacks
1	Eggs And Ham	Sirloin With Blue Cheese Compound Butter	Grilled Pesto Salmon With Asparagus	Banana Waffles
2	Italian Style Eggs	Bacon-Wrapped Beef Tenderloin	Cheddar-Stuffed Burgers With Zucchini	Keto Cinnamon Coffee
3	Orange And Dates Granola	Italian Beef Burgers	Chicken Cordon Bleu With Cauliflower	Keto Waffles and Blueberries
4	Bacon Muffins	Cheeseburger Casserole	Sesame-Crusted Tuna With Green Beans	Mushroom Omelet
5	Parsley And Pear Smoothie	Bacon-Wrapped Meatloaf	Rosemary Roasted Pork With Cauliflower Chicken Tikka With Cauliflower Rice	Chocolate Sea Salt Smoothie
6	Peach And Coconut Smoothie	Keto Cheesesteak Casserole	Grilled Salmon And Zucchini With Mango Sauce	Zucchini Lasagna
7	Bacon And Egg Breakfast Sandwich	Slow Cooker Balsamic Roast Beef	Slow-Cooker Pot Roast With Green Beans	Vegan Keto Scramble

Week 2

Day	Breakfast	Lunch	Dinner	Snacks
1	Korma Curry	Greek Style Lamb Chops	Beef And Broccoli Stir-Fry	Parmesan Cheese Strips
2	Zucchini Bars	Asian Beef Short Ribs	Parmesan-Crusted Halibut With Asparagus	Peanut Butter Power Granola
3	Mushroom Soup	Buffalo Turkey Balls	Hearty Beef And Bacon Casserole	Homemade Graham Crackers
4	Stuffed Portobello Mushrooms	Coconut Chicken	Sesame Wings With Cauliflower	Keto No-Bake Cookies
5	Lettuce Salad	Buffalo Drumsticks With Chili Aioli	Chicken Pan with Veggies and Pesto	Swiss Cheese Crunchy Nachos
6	Onion Soup	Cucumber Avocado Salad with Bacon	Cabbage Soup with Beef	Healthy Keto Green Smoothie
7	Asparagus Salad	Bacon Cheeseburger Soup	Cauliflower Rice Soup with Chicken	Healthy Zucchini & Beef Frittata

Week 3

Day	Breakfast	Lunch	Dinner	Snacks
1	Cheesy Breakfast Muffins	Ham and Provolone Sandwich	Quick Pumpkin Soup	Avocado-Raspberry Smoothie
2	Spinach, Mushroom, and Goat Cheese Frittata	Bacon-Wrapped Beef Tenderloin	Cheddar-Stuffed Burgers With Zucchini	Almond-Strawberry Smoothie
3	Green Vegetable Quiche	Italian Beef Burgers	Chicken Cordon Bleu With Cauliflower	Keto Waffles and Blueberries
4	Cheesy Broccoli Muffins	Cheeseburger Casserole	Sesame-Crusted Tuna With Green Beans	Mushroom Omelet
5	Berry Chocolate Breakfast Bowl	Bacon-Wrapped Meatloaf	Rosemary Roasted Pork With Cauliflower Chicken Tikka With Cauliflower Rice	Chocolate Sea Salt Smoothie
6	"Coco-Nut" Granola	Keto Cheesesteak Casserole	Grilled Salmon And Zucchini With Mango Sauce	Zucchini Lasagna
7	Bacon Artichoke Omelet	Slow Cooker Balsamic Roast Beef	Slow-Cooker Pot Roast With Green Beans	Vegan Keto Scramble

Week 4

Day	Breakfast	Lunch	Dinner	Snacks
1	Eggs And Ham	Greek Style Lamb Chops	Creamy Garlic Chicken	Healthy Zucchini & Beef Frittata
2	Italian Style Eggs	Asian Beef Short Ribs	Parmesan-Crusted Halibut With Asparagus	Grilled Chicken & Avocado Power Salad with Lemon Tahini Dressing
3	Orange And Dates Granola	Buffalo Turkey Balls	Hearty Beef And Bacon Casserole	Spiced Turkey Served with Avocado Relish
4	Bacon Muffins	Coconut Chicken	Sesame Wings With Cauliflower	Keto No-Bake Cookies
5	Parsley And Pear Smoothie	Buffalo Drumsticks With Chili Aioli	Chicken Pan with Veggies and Pesto	Swiss Cheese Crunchy Nachos
6	Peach And Coconut Smoothie	Cucumber Avocado Salad with Bacon	Cabbage Soup with Beef	Healthy Keto Green Smoothie
7	Bacon And Egg Breakfast Sandwich	Bacon Cheeseburger Soup	Cauliflower Rice Soup with Chicken	Healthy Zucchini & Beef Frittata

CHAPTER 7.
Tips on Losing Weight on Keto After 50

EXERCISE

In the fitness world, it is already established that 80% of your weight loss success comes from the diet. So just by following the Keto diet alone, you are already making great progress. However, if you want that extra edge in your weight loss, consider doing exercises.

You have plenty of options here. You can do cardio exercises such as jogging, running, or cycling every morning for 30 minutes, but strength training works just as well for older adults. You should do both if you can.

Cardio exercises can get the heart pumping and get the body moving more freely, but note that your muscle mass starts to decline after 50. So work on your muscles as well.

TEAM UP

A group activity is always more entertaining. So if you can find like-minded individuals who are also into Keto diets, consider doing it together with them. It makes things much easier. This tip also applies to some other tips that I will show you, such as the exercise that I just covered.

MOVE MORE

Moving more here does not mean more cardio exercises. You cannot expect to get any more effective weight loss if you exercise for 30mns a day and then sit on the couch for the rest of the day. The idea is to burn more calories than you can take in, so it pays to be a little extra active throughout the day.

If you have a desk job, consider getting up at least once an hour and take a short break by walking in the lobby for at least 5 minutes. It doesn't seem much, but it helps in the long run.

MORE PROTEIN

Protein is very important for both weight loss and youth, including the protection against muscle degradation and other aging ailments. Couple a high protein intake with strength exercise, and you can be sure that you would be building muscles faster than they can degrade. You won't look like Arnold when he was a bodybuilder, but you might even look fitter than the guy in his 20s at your workplace.

TALK TO A DIETITIAN
The first thing you should do before getting into any diet is to consult your dietitian. While the Keto diet works for many people, you never really know if it will work for you. Therefore, it is wise to ask your dietitian first before you jump in, rather than suffer some adverse effects because your body is not compatible with this diet.

COOK AT HOME MORE
Or eat out less frequently. There are two reasons why you should do that. For one, there are only a few places, if at all, that serve Keto-based foods, let alone those that follow your diet plan. You need to prepare your food if you want to do a Keto diet. Another benefit is economics. You will buy most of your ingredients and prepare your meals ahead of time. This means you will only spend your money on the ingredients you know you will need.

EAT MORE PRODUCE
While we are on the subject of eating, consider incorporating more produces in your diet, some of which I have covered already. Vegetables and fruits are full of nutrients that your body needs to remain healthy, so it should be included in your diet.

HIRE A PERSONAL TRAINER
While we are still discussing exercising, consider getting yourself a personal trainer. That way, you can get the most out of your exercises, and your trainer also doubles as an exercise partner as well because they hold you accountable for your commitments. Your trainer is very helpful when you do strength training because they can teach you how to perform the exercise with the correct form and to prevent you from injuring yourself.

RELY LESS ON CONVENIENCE FOODS
Convenient foods are convenient but not healthy. Not by a long shot. They are rich in calories and often do not pack essential nutrients such as protein, fiber, vitamins, etc. If you can, ditch inconvenient foods altogether.

FIND AN ACTIVITY YOU ENJOY
When you have done enough exercise, you will know what activities you like. One way to encourage yourself to exercise more regularly is by making it entertaining than a chore. If possible, stick to your favorite activities, and you can get the most out of your exercises. Keep in mind that the activities you enjoy may not be effective or needed, so you need to find other exercises to compensate, which you may not enjoy so much. For instance, if you like jogging, then you can work your leg muscles, but your arms are not involved. So you need to do pushups or other strength training exercises.

Here, your trainer can help you decide and create a workout routine that you can stick with as well.

CHECK WITH A HEALTHCARE PROVIDER
As mentioned earlier, the Keto diet works for many people, but it isn't for everyone. Your dietitian can tell you whether the Keto diet would work. However, it helps to check in with your healthcare provider to ensure that you do not have any medical condition that prevents you from losing weight, such as hypothyroidism and polycystic ovarian syndrome. It helps to know well in advance whether your body is even capable of losing fat in the first place before you commit and see no result, right.

HYDRATE PROPERLY

That means drinking enough water or herbal tea and ditch sweetened beverages or other drinks that contain sugar altogether. Making the transition will be difficult for the first few weeks, but your body will be thanking you for it. There is nothing healthier than good old plain water, and the recommended amount is 2 gallons a day. However, because you are on a Keto diet, your body needs to use up more water, so consider 2 gallons to the absolute minimum amount of water you need to drinks. I recommend you drink between 3 or even 4 gallons a day when you are on a Keto diet. If you get thirsty, then it is a sign of dehydration, so drink some water. Drinking plenty of water also leads to additional calories burned. You can shave off a few more calories by drinking cold water because your body will spend more energy trying to regulate your body temperature.

SUPPLEMENTS

When you get older, your body starts to lose its ability to absorb certain nutrients, which leads to deficits. For example, vitamin B12 and folate are some of the most common nutrients that people over 50 lack. They have an impact on your mood, energy level, and weight loss rate.

Therefore, if you feel tired when you are on your Keto diet, perhaps you do not get enough nutrients that your body needs. That does not mean you should eat more, no. You just need to take the right supplements.

GET ENOUGH SLEEP

When you are over 50, your body starts to fail you. You no longer have the ability to party past midnight without feeling horrible for the rest of the month. If there is the most crucial time to get 8 hours of sleep a day, then it is right now.

Getting enough sleep helps your body regulate the hormones in your body, so try to aim for 7 to 9 hours of sleep a day. You can get more restful sleep by creating a nighttime routine that involves not looking at a computer, phone, or TV screen for at least 1 hour before bed. You can drink warm milk or water to help your body relax or even do 10 to 20 minutes of stretching so you can get a restful sleep.

While we are on the subject of sleeping, try to maintain a consistent sleeping schedule. I understand that you want to sleep and wake up 1 to 4 hours later than usual during the weekend. But you want to go to bed and wake up at the same time, your mood and energy level will be higher. An added benefit is that your body will learn to wake up on its own even without the alarm.

MINDFUL EATING

Mindfulness isn't restricted to meditation alone. Again, we will not go over meditation in this guidebook because it is another topic altogether. But what you can do here is learn to love and appreciate your food. It sounds obnoxious, but it helps your mood and promotes weight loss.

Simply put, you just have to put away your phone and take away any other sources of distractions and focus solely on your food, how it tastes, etc. That means eating slowly. You will learn to appreciate how tasty your food is because you focus on eating.

How does this translate to weight loss? You see, there is a system in your body that determines how full you are. The issue here is that this system is not instantaneous. It takes some time to measure how full your stomach is before sending the signal to your brain. So when you eat too quickly, by the time you feel full, you would have already overshot by a country mile. If you eat slowly, your body has enough time to register your fullness bite by bite. So when you feel full, you have not overeaten.

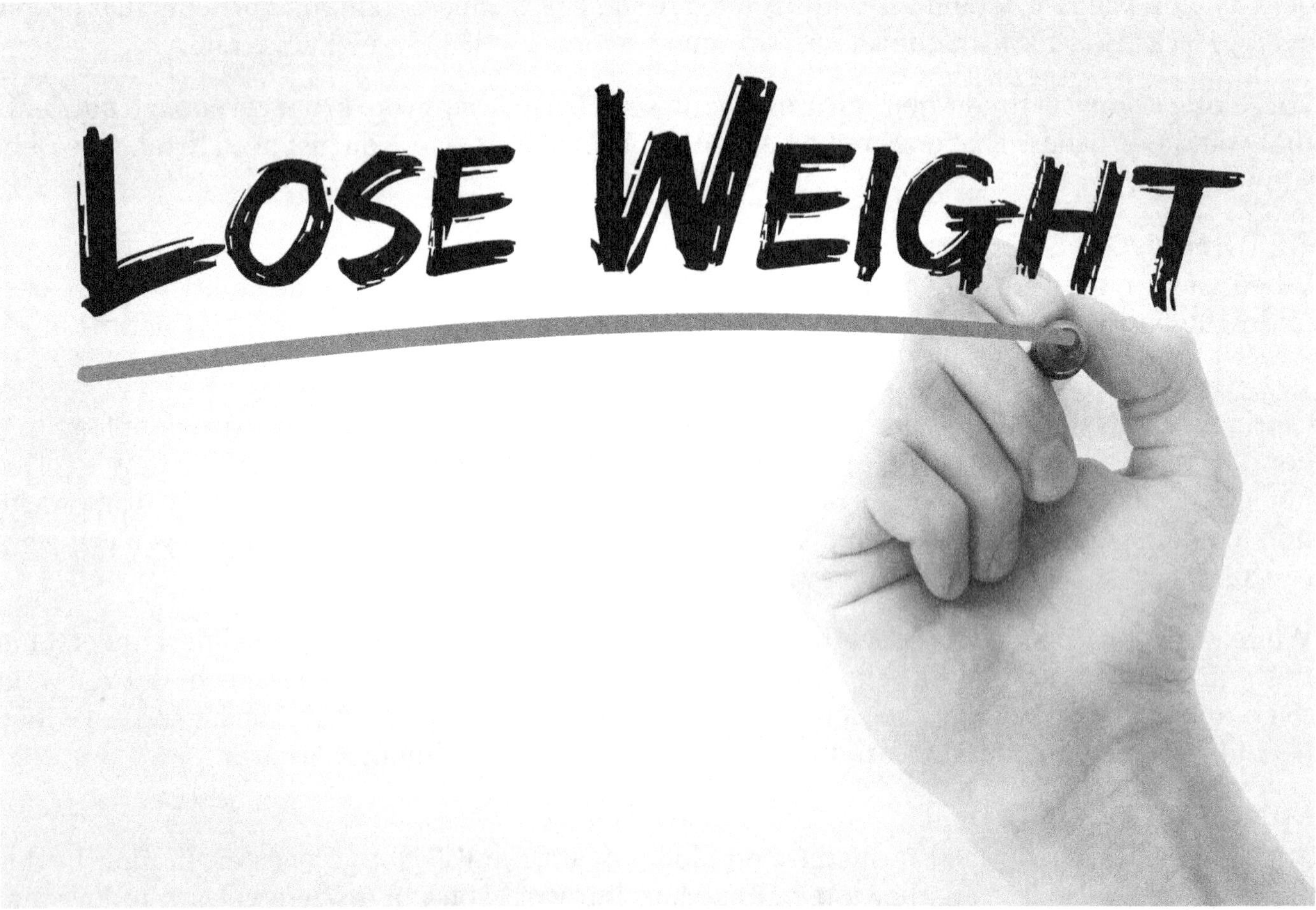
LOSE WEIGHT

CHAPTER 8.
Breakfast Recipes

Eggs and Ham

Preparation:
25 Minutes

Cooking:
15 Minutes

Servings:
4

Directions

1. Grease a muffin pan with melted ghee.
2. Divide ham slices each muffin mold to form your cups. In a bowl; mix eggs with scallions, pepper, and paprika and whisk well.
3. Divide this mix on top of the ham, introduce your ham cups in the oven at 400 °F and bake for 15 minutes. Leave cups to cool down before dividing on plates and serving.

Ingredients

- 4 eggs
- 10 ham slices
- 4 tbsp. of scallions
- A pinch of black pepper
- A pinch of sweet paprika
- 1 tbsp. of melted ghee

Nutritions: Calories: 250, Fat: 10g, Fiber: 3g, Carbs: 6g, Protein: 12g

Italian Style Eggs

Preparation:
20 Minutes

Cooking:
25 Minutes

Servings:
1

Directions

1. Heat up a pan with the oil over medium-high heat, add water, kale, rosemary, and tomatoes, stir; cover, and cook for 4 minutes.
2. Uncover the pan, stir again, and add eggs.
3. Stir and scramble eggs for 3 minutes.
4. Add vinegar, stir everything, and transfer to a serving plate. Top with chopped avocado and serve.

Ingredients

- 2 eggs
- 1/4 tsp. of rosemary; dried
- 1/2 cup of cherry tomatoes halved
- 1 1/2 cups of kale; chopped
- 1/2 tsp. of coconut oil
- 3 tbsp. of water
- 1 tsp. of balsamic vinegar
- 1/4 avocado; peeled and chopped

Nutritions: *Calories: 185, Fat: 10g, Fiber: 1g, Carbs: 6g, Protein: 7g*

Orange and Dates Granola

Preparation:
25 Minutes

Cooking:
15 Minutes

Servings:
6

Ingredients

- 5 oz. dates; soaked in hot water
- 1/2 cup pumpkin seeds
- Juice from 1 orange
- Grated rind of 1/2 orange
- 1 cup of desiccated coconut
- 1/2 cup of slivered almonds
- 1/2 cup of linseeds
- 1/2 cup of sesame seeds
- Almond milk for serving

Directions

1. In a bowl; mix almonds with orange rind, orange juice, linseeds, and coconut, pumpkin, and sesame seeds and stir well.
2. Drain dates, add them to your food processor and blend well. Add this paste to almonds mix and stir well again.
3. Spread this on a lined baking sheet, introduce in the oven at 350 °F and bake for 15 minutes, stirring every 4 minutes.
4. Take granola out of the oven, leave aside to cool down a bit and then serve with almond milk.

Nutritions: Calories: 208g, Protein: 6g, Fiber: 5, Fat: 9, Sugar: 0

Bacon Muffins

Preparation:
40 Minutes

Cooking:
20 Minutes

Servings:
4

Ingredients

- 4 oz. bacon slices
- 3 garlic cloves; minced
- 1 small yellow onion; chopped
- 1 zucchini; thinly sliced
- A handful of spinach; torn
- 6 canned and pickled artichoke hearts; chopped
- 8 eggs
- 1/4 tsp. paprika
- A pinch of black pepper
- A pinch of cayenne pepper
- 1/4 cup of coconut cream

Directions

1. Heat up a pan over medium-high heat, add bacon, stir; cook until it's crispy, transfer to paper towels, drain grease and leave aside for now.
2. Heat up the same pan over medium heat again, add garlic and onion, stir and cook for 4 minutes.
3. In a bowl; mix eggs with coconut cream, onions, garlic, paprika, black pepper, and cayenne and whisk well.
4. Add spinach, zucchini, and artichoke pieces and stir everything.
5. Divide crispy bacon slices in a muffin pan, add the egg mixture on top, introduce your muffins in the oven, and bake at 400 °F for 20 minutes. Leave them to cool down before serving them for breakfast.

Nutritions: Calories: 270, Fat: 12g, Fiber: 4g, Carbs: 6g, Protein: 12g

Parsley and Pear Smoothie

Preparation:
5 Minutes

Cooking:
0 Minutes

Servings:
6

Directions

1. In your kitchen blender, mix parsley with avocado, apple pear, pear, green apple, Granny Smith apple, plums, and bananas and blend very well.
2. Add ice and water and blend again very well. Transfer to tall glasses and serve right away.

Ingredients

- 1 apple pear; chopped
- 1 bunch of parsley; roughly chopped
- 1 small avocado; stoned and peeled
- 1 pear; peeled and chopped
- 1 green apple; chopped
- 1 Granny Smith apple; chopped
- 6 bananas; peeled and roughly chopped
- 2 plums; stoned
- 1 cup of ice
- 1 cup of water

Nutritions: *Calories: 208g, Carbs: 48g, Fiber: 13, Fat: 3g, Protein: 3, Sugar: 28*

Peach and Coconut Smoothie

Preparation:
5 Minutes

Cooking:
0 Minutes

Servings:
2

Directions

1. In your kitchen blender, mix coconut milk with ice and peaches and pulse a few times.
2. Add lemon zest to the taste and 1 drop lemon essential oil and pulse a few more times. Pour into glasses and serve right away.

Ingredients

- 1 cup of ice
- 2 peaches; peeled and chopped
- Lemon zest to the taste
- 1 cup of cold coconut milk
- 1 drop lemon essential oil

Nutritions: Calories: 200, Fat: 5g, Fiber: 4g, Carbs: 6g, Protein: 8g

Bacon and Egg Breakfast Sandwich

Preparation:
20 Minutes

Cooking:
8 Minutes

Servings:
2

Directions

1. Heat up a pan with the oil over medium-high heat, add bell peppers, stir and cook until they are soft.
2. Heat up another pan over medium heat, add bacon, stir and cook until it's crispy.
3. In a bowl; whisk eggs really well and add them to bell peppers.
4. Cook until eggs are done for about 8 minutes. Divide half of the bacon slices between plates, add eggs, top with bacon slices, and serve.

Ingredients

- 2 cups of bell peppers; chopped
- 1/2 tbsp. of avocado oil
- 3 eggs
- 4 bacon slices

Nutritions: *Calories: 200, Fat: 4g, Fiber: 3g, Carbs: 6g, Protein: 10g*

Korma Curry

Preparation:
10 Minutes

Cooking:
25 Minutes

Servings:
6

Ingredients

- 3-pound chicken breast, skinless, boneless
- 1 teaspoon of garam masala
- 1 teaspoon of curry powder
- 1 tablespoon of apple cider vinegar
- 1/2 cup of coconut cream
- 1 cup of organic almond milk
- 1 teaspoon of ground coriander
- ¾ teaspoon of ground cardamom
- 1/2 teaspoon of ginger powder
- 1/4 teaspoon of cayenne pepper
- ¾ teaspoon of ground cinnamon
- 1 tomato, diced
- 1 teaspoon of avocado oil
- 1/2 cup of water

Directions

1. Chop the chicken breast and put it in the saucepan.
2. Add avocado oil and start to cook it over medium heat.
3. Sprinkle the chicken with garam masala, curry powder, apple cider vinegar, ground coriander, cardamom, ginger powder, cayenne pepper, ground cinnamon, and diced tomato. Mix up the ingredients carefully. Cook them for 10 minutes.
4. Add water, coconut cream, and almond milk. Sauté the meat for 10 minutes more.

Nutritions: *Calories 411, fat 19.3, fiber 0.9, carbs 6, protein 49.9*

Zucchini Bars

Preparation:
10 Minutes

Cooking:
15 Minutes

Servings:
8

Ingredients

- 3 zucchini, grated
- 1/2 white onion, diced
- 2 teaspoons of butter
- 3 eggs, whisked
- 4 tablespoons of coconut flour
- 1 teaspoon of salt
- 1/2 teaspoon of ground black pepper
- 5 oz. of goat cheese, crumbled
- 4 oz. of Swiss cheese, shredded
- 1/2 cup of spinach, chopped
- 1 teaspoon of baking powder
- 1/2 teaspoon of lemon juice

Directions

1. In the mixing bowl, mix up together grated zucchini, diced onion, eggs, coconut flour, salt, ground black pepper, crumbled cheese, chopped spinach, baking powder, and lemon juice.
2. Add butter and churn the mixture until homogenous.
3. Line the baking dish with baking paper.
4. Transfer the zucchini mixture into the baking dish and flatten it.
5. Preheat the oven to 365F and put the dish inside.
6. Cook it for 15 minutes. Then chill the meal well.
7. Cut it into bars.

Nutritions: *Calories 199, Fat 1316, Fiber 215, Carbs 7.1, Protein 13.1*

Mushroom Soup

Preparation:
10 Minutes

Cooking:
25 Minutes

Servings:
4

Ingredients

- 1 cup of water
- 1 cup of coconut milk
- 1 cup of white mushrooms, chopped
- 1/2 carrot, chopped
- 1/4 white onion, diced
- 1 tablespoon of butter
- 2 oz. turnip, chopped
- 1 teaspoon of dried dill
- 1/2 teaspoon of ground black pepper
- ¾ teaspoon of smoked paprika
- 1 oz. of celery stalk, chopped

Directions

1. Pour water and coconut milk into the saucepan. Bring the liquid to boil.
2. Add chopped mushrooms, carrot, and turnip. Close the lid and boil for 10 minutes.
3. Meanwhile, put butter in the skillet. Add diced onion. Sprinkle it with dill, ground black pepper, and smoked paprika. Roast the onion for 3 minutes.
4. Add the roasted onion to the soup mixture.
5. Then add chopped celery stalk. Close the lid.
6. Cook soup for 10 minutes.
7. Then ladle it into the serving bowls.

Nutritions: Calories 181, fat 17.3, fiber 2.5, carbs 6.9, protein 2.4

Stuffed Portobello Mushrooms

Preparation:
10 Minutes

Cooking:
10 Minutes

Servings:
4

Ingredients

- 2 Portobello mushrooms
- 1 cup of spinach, chopped, steamed
- 2 oz. of artichoke hearts, drained, chopped
- 1 tablespoon of coconut cream
- 1 tablespoon of cream cheese
- 1 teaspoon of minced garlic
- 1 tablespoon of fresh cilantro, chopped
- 3 oz. of Cheddar cheese, grated
- 1/2 teaspoon of ground black pepper
- 2 tablespoons of olive oil
- 1/2 teaspoon of salt

Directions

1. Sprinkle mushrooms with olive oil and place in the tray.
2. Transfer the tray to the preheated to 360F oven and broil them for 5 minutes.
3. Meanwhile, blend together artichoke hearts, coconut cream, cream cheese, minced garlic, and chopped cilantro.
4. Add grated cheese to the mixture and sprinkle with ground black pepper and salt.
5. Fill the broiled mushrooms with the cheese mixture and cook them for 5 minutes more. Serve the mushrooms only hot.

Nutritions: Calories 183, fat 16.3, fiber 1.9, carbs 3, protein 7.7

Lettuce Salad

Preparation:
10 Minutes

Cooking:
-

Servings:
1

Directions

1. Place lettuce in the salad bowl. Add chopped seitan and shredded cheese.
2. Then chop the egg roughly and add in the salad bowl too.
3. Mix up together lemon juice with the avocado oil.
4. Sprinkle the salad with the oil mixture and sunflower seeds. Don't stir the salad before serving.

Ingredients

- 1 cup of Romaine lettuce, roughly chopped
- 3 oz. of seitan, chopped
- 1 tablespoon of avocado oil
- 1 teaspoon of sunflower seeds
- 1 teaspoon of lemon juice
- 1 egg, boiled, peeled
- 2 oz. of Cheddar cheese, shredded

Nutritions: *Calories 663, Fat 29.5, Fiber 4.7, Carbs 3.8, Protein 84.2*

Onion Soup

Preparation:
10 Minutes

Cooking:
25 Minutes

Servings:
4

Directions

1. Put butter in the saucepan and melt it.
2. Add diced white onion, chili flakes, and garlic powder. Mix it up and sauté for 10 minutes over medium-low heat.
3. Then add water, heavy cream, and chopped mushrooms. Close the lid.
4. Cook the soup for 15 minutes more.
5. Then blend the soup until you get the creamy texture. Ladle it in the bowls.

Ingredients

- 2 cups of white onion, diced
- 4 tablespoon of butter
- 1/2 cup of white mushrooms, chopped
- 3 cups of water
- 1 cup of heavy cream
- 1 teaspoon of salt
- 1 teaspoon of chili flakes
- 1 teaspoon of garlic powder

Nutritions: Calories 155, Fat 15.1, Fiber 0.9, Carbs 4.7, Protein 1.2

Asparagus Salad

Preparation:
10 Minutes

Cooking:
15 Minutes

Servings:
3

Ingredients

- 10 oz. of asparagus
- 1 tablespoon of olive oil
- 1/2 teaspoon of white pepper
- 4 oz. of Feta cheese, crumbled
- 1 cup of lettuce, chopped
- 1 tablespoon of canola oil
- 1 teaspoon of apple cider vinegar
- 1 tomato, diced

Directions

1. Preheat the oven to 365F.
2. Place asparagus in the tray, sprinkle with olive oil and white pepper, and transfer to the preheated oven. Cook it for 15 minutes.
3. Meanwhile, put crumbled Feta in the salad bowl.
4. Add chopped lettuce and diced tomato.
5. Sprinkle the ingredients with apple cider vinegar.
6. Chill the cooked asparagus to room temperature and add in the salad.
7. Shake the salad gently before serving.

Nutritions: *calories 207, fat 17.6, fiber 2.4, carbs 6.8, protein 7.8*

Cheesy Breakfast Muffins

Preparation:
15 Minutes

Cooking:
12 Minutes

Servings:
6

Ingredients

- 4 tablespoons of melted butter
- 3/4 tablespoon of baking powder
- 1 cup of almond flour
- 2 large eggs, lightly beaten
- 2 ounces cream cheese mixed with 2 tablespoons heavy whipping cream
- A handful of shredded Mexican blend cheese

Directions

1. Preheat the oven to 400°F. Grease 6 muffin tin cups with melted butter and set aside.
2. Combine the baking powder and almond flour in a bowl. Stir well and set aside.
3. Stir together four tablespoons of melted butter, eggs, shredded cheese, and cream cheese in a separate bowl.
4. The egg and the dry mixture must be combined using a hand mixer to beat until it is creamy and well blended.
5. The mixture must be scooped into the greased muffin cups evenly.
6. Baking time: 12 minutes

Nutritions: *Calories: 214, Fat: 15.6g, Fiber: 3.1g, Carbohydrates: 5.1 g, Protein: 9.5 g*

Spinach, Mushroom, and Goat Cheese Frittata

Preparation:
15 Minutes

Cooking:
20 Minutes

Servings:
5

Ingredients

- 2 tablespoons of olive oil
- 1 cup of fresh mushrooms, sliced
- 6 bacon slices, cooked and chopped
- 1 cup of spinach, shredded
- 10 large eggs, beaten
- 1/2 cup of goat cheese, crumbled
- Pepper and salt

Directions

1. Preheat the oven to 350°F.
2. Heat oil and add the mushrooms and fry for 3 minutes until they start to brown, stirring frequently.
3. Fold in the bacon and spinach and cook for about 1 to 2 minutes, or until the spinach is wilted.
4. Slowly pour in the beaten eggs and cook for 3 to 4 minutes. Making use of a spatula, lift the edges for allowing uncooked egg to flow underneath.
5. Top with the goat cheese, and then sprinkle the salt and pepper to season.
6. Bake in the preheated oven for about 15 minutes until lightly golden brown around the edges.

Nutritions: Calories: 265, Fat: 11.6g, Fiber: 8.6g, Carbohydrates: 5.1 g, Protein: 12.9g

Yogurt Waffles

Preparation:
15 Minutes

Cooking:
25 Minutes

Servings:
5

Ingredients

- 1/2 cup golden flax seeds meal
- 1/2 cup plus 3 tablespoons almond flour
- 1-11/2 tablespoons granulated Erythritol
- 1 tablespoon unsweetened vanilla whey protein powder
- 1/4 teaspoon baking soda
- 1/2 teaspoon organic baking powder
- 1/4 teaspoon xanthan gum
- Salt, as required
- 1 large organic egg, white and yolk separated
- 1 organic whole egg
- 2 tablespoons unsweetened almond milk
- 11/2 tablespoons unsalted butter
- 3 ounces plain Greek yogurt

Directions

1. Preheat the waffle iron and then grease it.
2. In a large bowl, add the flour, Erythritol, protein powder, baking soda, baking powder, xanthan gum, salt, and mix until well combined.
3. In another bowl or container, put in the egg white and beat until stiff peaks form.
4. In a third bowl, add two egg yolks, whole egg, almond milk, butter, yogurt, and beat until well combined.
5. Place egg mixture into the bowl of the flour mixture and mix until well combined.
6. Gently, fold in the beaten egg whites.
7. Place 1/4 cup of the mixture into preheated waffle iron and cook for about 4–5 minutes or until golden brown.
8. Repeat with the remaining mixture.
9. Serve warm.

Nutritions: Calories: 265, Fat: 11.5g, Fiber: 9.5g, Carbohydrates: 5.2g, Protein: 7.5g

Green Vegetable Quiche

Preparation:
20 Minutes

Cooking:
20 Minutes

Servings:
4

Ingredients

- 6 organic eggs
- 1/2 cup unsweetened almond milk
- Salt and ground black pepper, as required
- 2 cups fresh baby spinach, chopped
- 1/2 cup green bell pepper, seeded and chopped
- 1 scallion, chopped
- 1/4 cup fresh cilantro, chopped
- 1 tablespoon fresh chives, minced
- 3 tablespoons mozzarella cheese, grated

Directions

1. Preheat your oven to 400°F.
2. Lightly grease a pie dish.
3. In a bowl, add eggs, almond milk, salt, and black pepper, and beat until well combined. Set aside.
4. In another bowl, add the vegetables and herbs and mix well.
5. At the bottom of the prepared pie dish, place the veggie mixture evenly and top with the egg mixture.
6. Let the quiche bake for about 20 minutes.
7. Remove the pie dish from the oven and immediately sprinkle with the Parmesan cheese.
8. Set aside for about 5 minutes before slicing.
9. Cut into desired sized wedges and serve warm.

Nutritions: Calories: 298, Fat: 10.4g, Fiber: 5.9g, Carbohydrates: 4.1 g, Protein: 7.9g

Cheesy Broccoli Muffins

Preparation:
15 Minutes

Cooking:
20 Minutes

Servings:
6

Ingredients
- 2 tablespoons unsalted butter
- 6 large organic eggs
- 1/2 cup heavy whipping cream
- 1/2 cup Parmesan cheese, grated
- Salt and ground black pepper, as required
- 1 1/4 cups broccoli, chopped
- 2 tablespoons fresh parsley, chopped
- 1/2 cup Swiss cheese, grated

Directions
1. Grease a 12-cup muffin tin.
2. In a bowl or container, put in the cream, eggs, Parmesan cheese, salt, and black pepper, and beat until well combined.
3. Divide the broccoli and parsley in the bottom of each prepared muffin cup evenly.
4. Top with the egg mixture, followed by the Swiss cheese.
5. Let the muffins bake for about 20 minutes, rotating the pan once halfway through.
6. Carefully, invert the muffins onto a serving platter and serve warm.

Nutritions: Calories: 241, Fat: 11.5g, Fiber: 8.5g, Carbohydrates: 4.1 g, Protein: 11.1g

Berry Chocolate Breakfast Bowl

Preparation:
10 Minutes

Cooking:
0 Minutes

Servings:
2

Directions

1. The berries must be divided into four bowls, pour on the almond milk.
2. Drizzle with the maple syrup and sprinkle the cocoa powder on top, a tablespoon per bowl.
3. Top with the cashew nuts and enjoy immediately.

Ingredients

- 1/2 cup strawberries, fresh or frozen
- 1/2 cup blueberries, fresh or frozen
- 1 cup unsweetened almond milk
- Sugar-free maple syrup to taste
- 2 tbsp. unsweetened cocoa powder
- 1 tbsp. cashew nuts for topping

Nutritions: Calories: 287, Fat: 5.9g, Fiber: 11.4g, Carbohydrates: 3.1 g, Protein: 4.2g

"Coco-Nut" Granola

Preparation:
10 Minutes

Cooking:
60 Minutes

Servings:
8

Directions

1. Preheat the oven to 250°F. Line 2 baking sheets with parchment paper. Set aside.
2. Toss all the ingredients together.
3. The granola will then put into baking sheets and spread it out evenly.
4. Bake the granola for about 1 hr.

Ingredients

- 2 cups shredded unsweetened coconut
- 1 cup sliced almonds
- 1 cup raw sunflower seeds
- 1/2 cup raw pumpkin seeds
- 1/2 cup walnuts
- 1/2 cup melted coconut oil
- 10 drops liquid stevia
- 1 teaspoon ground cinnamon
- 1/2 teaspoon ground nutmeg

Nutritions: Calories: 131, Fat: 4.1g, Fiber: 5.8g, Carbohydrates: 2.8 g, Protein: 5.6 g

Bacon Artichoke Omelet

Preparation:
10 Minutes

Cooking:
10 Minutes

Servings:
4

Ingredients

- 6 eggs, beaten
- 2 tablespoons heavy (whipping) cream
- 8 bacon slices, cooked and chopped
- 1 tablespoon olive oil
- 1/4 cup chopped onion
- 1/2 cup chopped artichoke hearts (canned, packed in water)
- Sea salt
- Freshly ground black pepper

Directions

1. In a bowl or container, the eggs, heavy cream, and bacon must be mixed.
2. Heat olive oil then sauté the onion until tender, about 3 minutes.
3. Pour the egg mixture into the skillet for 1 minute.
4. Cook the omelet, lifting the edges with a spatula to let the uncooked egg flow underneath, for 2 minutes.
5. Sprinkle the artichoke hearts on top and flip the omelet.
6. Cook for 4 minutes more until the egg is firm.
7. Flip the omelet over again, so the artichoke hearts are on top.
8. Remove from the heat, cut the omelet into quarters, and season with salt and black pepper.
9. Transfer the omelet to plates and serve.

Nutritions: Calories: 314, Fat: 7.1g, Fiber: 5.4g, Carbohydrates: 3.1 g, Protein: 8.5g

Spinach-Mushroom Frittata

Preparation:
10 Minutes

Cooking:
15 Minutes

Servings:
6

Ingredients

- 2 tablespoons olive oil
- 1 cup sliced fresh mushrooms
- 1 cup shredded spinach
- 6 bacon slices, cooked and chopped
- 10 large eggs, beaten
- 1/2 cup crumbled goat cheese
- Sea salt
- Freshly ground black pepper

Directions

1. Preheat the oven to 350°F.
2. Heat olive oil and sauté the mushrooms until lightly browned about 3 minutes.
3. Add the spinach and bacon and sauté until the greens are wilted about 1 minute.
4. Add the eggs and cook, lifting the edges of the frittata with a spatula so uncooked egg flow underneath, for 3 to 4 minutes.
5. Sprinkle with crumbled goat cheese and season lightly with salt and pepper.
6. Bake until set and lightly browned, about 15 minutes.
7. Remove the frittata from the oven, and let it stand for 5 minutes.
8. Cut into six wedges and serve immediately.

Nutritions: *Calories: 312, Fat: 6.8g, Fiber: 5.1g, Carbohydrates: 3.1 g, Protein: 10.5g*

Crêpes with Lemon-Buttery Syrup

Preparation:
10 Minutes

Cooking:
20 Minutes

Servings:
6

Ingredients

- 6 ounces mascarpone cheese, softened
- 6 eggs
- 1 1/2 tbsp. granulated swerve
- 1/4 cup almond flour
- 1 tsp. baking soda
- 1 tsp. baking powder

For the Syrup

- 3/4 cup of water
- 2 tbsp. lemon juice
- 1 tbsp. butter
- 3/4 cup swerve, powdered
- 1 tbsp. vanilla extract
- 1/2 tsp. xanthan gum

Directions

1. With the use of an electric mixer, mix all crepes ingredients until well incorporated.
2. Use melted butter to grease a frying pan and set over medium heat; cook the crepes.
3. Flip over and cook the other side for a further 2 minutes; repeat the remaining batter.
4. Put the crepes on a plate.
5. In the same pan, mix swerve, butter and water; simmer for 6 minutes as you stir.
6. Transfer the mixture to a blender and a 1/4 teaspoon of xanthan gum and vanilla extract and mix well.
7. Place in the remaining 1/4 teaspoon of xanthan gum and allow sitting until the syrup is thick.

Nutritions: Calories: 312, Fat: 11.5g, Fiber: 3.8g, Carbohydrates: 2.4 g, Protein: 5.1g

Flaxseed, Maple & Pumpkin Muffin

Preparation:
10 Minutes

Cooking:
30 Minutes

Servings:
6

Ingredients

- 1 tbsp. cinnamon
- 1 cup pure pumpkin puree
- 1 tbsp. pumpkin pie spice
- 2 tbsp. coconut oil
- 1 egg
- 1/2 tbsp. baking powder
- 1/2 tsp. salt
- 1/2 tsp. apple cider vinegar
- 1/2 tsp. vanilla extract
- 1/3 cup erythritol
- 1 1/4 cup flaxseeds (ground)
- 1/4 cup Maple Syrup

Directions

1. Line ten muffin tins with ten muffin liners and preheat oven to 350oF.
2. All the ingredients must be blended until smooth and creamy, around 5 minutes.
3. Evenly divide batter into prepared muffin tins.
4. Pop in the oven and let it bake for 20 minutes or until tops are lightly browned.
5. Let it cool. Evenly divide into suggested servings and place in meal prep containers.

Nutritions: Calories: 241, Fat: 11.3g, Fiber: 15.9g, Carbohydrates: 3.1 g, Protein: 8.9g

Onion Cheese Muffins

Preparation:
15 Minutes

Cooking:
20 Minutes

Servings:
6

Directions
1. Line 6 muffin tins with six muffin liners. Set aside and preheat oven to 350oF.
2. In a bowl, stir the dry and wet ingredients alternately. Mix well.
3. Scoop a spoonful of the batter to the prepared muffin tins.
4. Bake for 20 minutes in the oven until golden brown.

Ingredients
- 1/4 cup Colby jack cheese, shredded
- 1/4 cup shallots, minced
- 1/2 tsp. salt
- 1 cup almond flour
- 1 egg
- 3 tbsp. melted butter
- 3 tbsp. sour cream

Nutritions: Calories: 241, Fat: 5.1g, Fiber: 2.6g, Carbohydrates: 3.1 g, Protein: 4.2 g

Cajun Crabmeat Frittata

Preparation: 15 Minutes

Cooking: 20 Minutes

Servings: 4

Ingredients

- 1 tbsp. olive oil
- 1 onion, chopped
- 4 ounces crabmeat, chopped
- 1 tsp. Cajun seasoning
- 6 large eggs, slightly beaten
- 1/2 cup Greek yogurt

Directions

1. Let the oven preheat to 350°F/175°C, then set a large skillet over medium heat and warm the oil.
2. Add in onion and sauté until soft; place in crabmeat and cook for two more minutes.
3. Season with Cajun seasoning.
4. Evenly distribute the ingredients at the bottom of the skillet.
5. Whisk the eggs with yogurt.
6. Transfer to the skillet.
7. Put it in the oven and let the frittata bake for about 18 minutes or until eggs are cooked.
8. Slice into wedges and serve warm.

Nutritions: *Calories: 256, Fat: 4.9g, Fiber: 2.9g, Carbohydrates: 3.1 g, Protein: 8.9g*

CHAPTER 9.
Lunch Recipes

Sirloin with Blue Cheese Compound

Preparation:
10 Minutes + 1h to chil

Cooking:
12 Minutes

Servings:
4

Ingredients

- 6 tbsp. butter, room temperature
- 4 ounces blue cheese
- 1 tbsp. olive oil
- 4 (5 ounces) beef sirloin steaks
- Sea salt
- Freshly ground black pepper

Directions

1. Set the steaks out until they reach room temperature. Set aside.
2. Place the butter in a blender and pulse until the butter is whipped, about 2 minutes.
3. Add the cheese and pulse until just incorporated.
4. Spoon the butter mixture onto a sheet of plastic wrap and roll it into a log about 1 1/2 inches in diameter by twisting both ends of the plastic wrap in opposite directions.
5. Refrigerate the butter until completely set, about 1 hour.
6. Slice the butter into 1/2 inch disks and set them on a plate in the refrigerator until you are ready to serve the steaks. Store leftover butter in the refrigerator for up to 1 week.
7. Rub the steaks all over with the olive oil and season them with salt and pepper.
8. Grill the steaks until they reach your desired doneness, about 6 minutes on each side for medium.
9. Let the steaks rest for 10 minutes. Serve each topped with a disk of the compound butter.

Nutritions: *Calories 544, Fat 44g, Protein 35g, Carbs 0g*

Bacon-Wrapped Beef Tenderloin

Preparation:
10 Minutes

Cooking:
15 Minutes

Servings:
4

Ingredients

- 4 (4ounce) beef tenderloin steaks
- Freshly ground black pepper
- 8 bacon slices
- 1 tbsp. extra-virgin olive oil Sea salt

Directions

1. Preheat the oven to 450°F.
2. Season the steaks with salt and pepper.
3. Wrap each steak snugly around the edges with 2 slices of bacon and secure the bacon with toothpicks.
4. Place a large skillet over medium-high heat and add the olive oil.
5. Pan sears the steaks for 4 minutes per side and transfer them to a baking sheet.
6. Roast the steaks until they reach your desired doneness, about 6 minutes for medium.
7. Remove the steaks from the oven and let them rest for 10 minutes.
8. Remove the toothpicks and serve.

Nutritions: *Calories 565, Fat 49g, Protein 28g, Carbs 0g*

Italian Beef Burgers

Preparation:
10 Minutes

Cooking:
12 Minutes

Servings:
4

Ingredients

- 1 pound 75% lean ground beef
- 1/4 cup ground almonds
- 2 tbsp. chopped fresh basil
- 1 tsp. minced garlic
- 1/4 tsp. sea salt
- 1 tbsp. olive oil
- 1 tomato cut into 4 thick slices
- 1/4 sweet onion, sliced thinly

Directions

1. In a medium bowl, mix together the ground beef, ground almonds, basil, garlic, and salt until well mixed.
2. Form the beef mixture into four equal patties and flatten them to about 1/2 inch thick.
3. Place a large skillet on medium-high heat and add the olive oil.
4. Panfry the burgers until cooked through, flipping them once, about 12 minutes in total.
5. Pat away excess grease with a paper towel and serve the burgers with a slice of tomato and onion.

Nutritions: *Calories 441: Fat 37g: Protein 22g: Carbs 4g*

Cheeseburger Casserole

Preparation:
10 Minutes

Cooking:
40 Minutes

Servings:
6

Ingredients

- 1 pound lean ground beef
- 1/2 cup chopped sweet onion
- 2 tsp. minced garlic
- 1 1/2 cups shredded aged Cheddar cheese
- 1 large tomato, chopped
- 1 tsp. minced fresh basil
- 1/4 tsp. sea salt
- Freshly ground black pepper
- 1/2 cup heavy (whipping) cream

Directions

1. Preheat the oven to 350°F.
2. Place a large skillet over medium-high heat and add the ground beef.
3. Brown the beef until cooked through, about 6 minutes.
4. Stir in the onion and garlic and cook until the vegetables are tender, about 4 minutes.
5. Transfer the beef and vegetables to an 8-by-8-inch casserole dish.
6. In a medium bowl, stir together 1 cup of shredded cheese and the heavy cream, tomato, basil, salt, and pepper until well combined.
7. Pour the cream mixture over the beef mixture and top the casserole with the remaining 1/2 cup of shredded cheese.
8. Bake until the casserole is bubbly and cheese is melted and lightly browned, about 30 minutes.
9. Serve.

Nutritions: *Calories 410, Fat 33g, Protein 20g, Carbs 3g*

Bacon-Wrapped Meatloaf

Preparation:
10 Minutes

Cooking:
1 Hours

Servings:
4

Ingredients
- 2 tbsp. butter
- 1 yellow onion, finely chopped
- 25 ounces of ground beef
- 1/2 cup heavy whipping cream
- 1/2 cup shredded cheese
- 7 ounces sliced bacon
- 1 egg
- 1 tbsp. dried oregano
- 1 tsp. sea salt
- 1/2 tsp. black pepper
- 1 1/4 cups heavy whipping cream (for gravy)
- 1/2 tbsp. soy sauce

Directions
1. Preheat oven to 400°F.
2. Fry the onion until soft but not browned.
3. Mix the ground beef in a bowl. Add all other ingredients, except the bacon. Mix well, but avoid overworking it.
4. Form into a loaf pan, then wrap with bacon.
5. Bake for approximately 45 minutes. If the bacon begins to overcook before the meat is done, cover with aluminum foil and lower the heat a bit.
6. Save the juices that accumulate in the baking dish and use them to make gravy. Mix the juices and heavy cream in a smaller saucepan.
7. Bring to a boil and lower heat, let simmer for 10 – 15 minutes until it has the right consistency. You can add the soy sauce for extra flavor.
8. Serve with freshly boiled broccoli or cauliflower with butter, salt, and pepper.

Nutritions: Calories 1038, Fat 90g, Protein 48g, Net carbs 6g

Keto Cheesesteak Casserole

Preparation:
10 Minutes

Cooking:
20 Minutes

Servings:
4

Ingredients

- 4 oz. butter
- 10 oz. mushrooms
- 1 yellow onion
- 2 green bell peppers
- 1 pound ribeye steak, thinly sliced
- 1 glove garlic
- 1 tbsp. Italian seasoning
- 1 tsp. chili flakes
- 7 oz. shredded provolone cheese
- Salt and pepper
- 4 tbsp. unsweetened marinara sauce
- 1/2 teaspoon of olive oil for drizzle
- Green leafies for topping

Directions

1. Preheat oven to 450°F.
2. Slice or chop mushrooms. Finely chop onion and bell pepper.
3. Fry the vegetables in butter until slightly soft. Put aside.
4. Slice the meat and fry in the same frying pan. Add the garlic and spices. Season with salt and pepper.
5. Return the veggies to the pan and stir.
6. Place everything in a greased baking dish and sprinkle the cheese on top.
7. Bake for 15 – 20 minutes or until the casserole turns golden brown.
8. Drizzle marinara sauce on top and serve with leafy greens and olive oil.

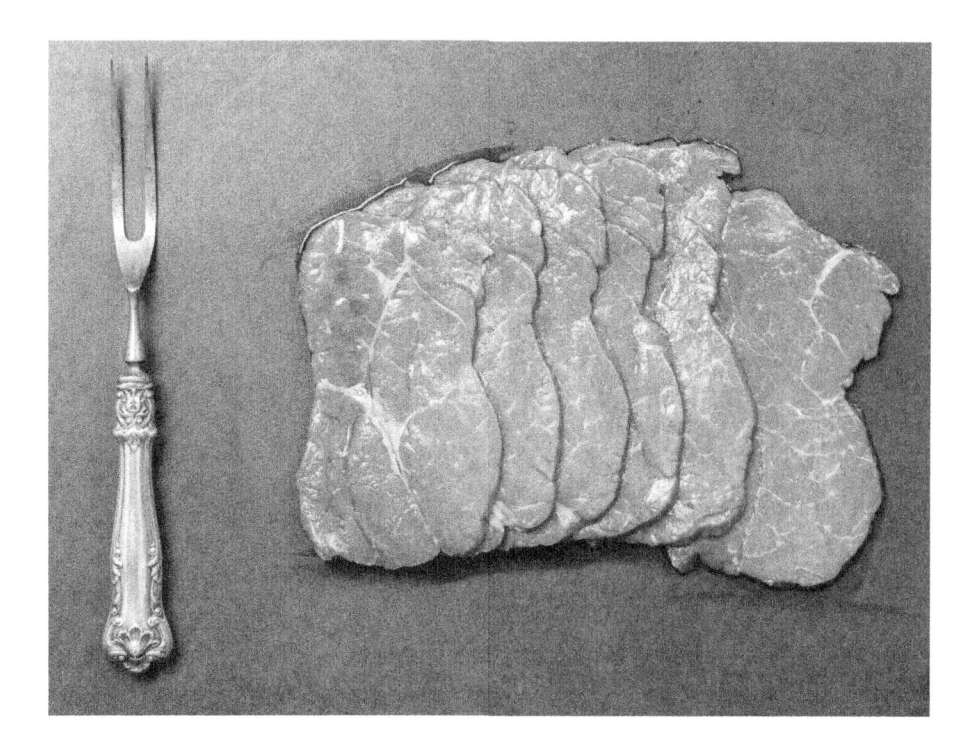

Nutritions: Calories 806, Fat 68g, Protein 40g, Carb 9g

Slow Cooker Balsamic Roast Beef

Preparation:
10 Minutes

Cooking:
8 Hours

Servings:
4

Directions

1. Place the roast beef in the slow cooker.
2. In a mixing bowl, mix all other ingredients and pour over the roast.
3. Let it sit in the slow cooker for six to eight hours.
4. Once cooked, remove from the slow cooker and break the meat apart.
5. You can add a dollop of sour cream and chopped scallions to top off each serving.

Ingredients

- 1 ¾ pound boneless round roast
- 1 cup beef broth
- 1 tbsp. stevia
- 1 tbsp. soy sauce
- 1 tbsp. Worcestershire sauce
- 4 cloves garlic, chopped
- 1/4 tsp. red pepper flakes

Nutritions: Calories 355: Protein 59g: Fat 9.7g: Carbohydrates 8g

Greek Style Lamb Chops

Preparation:
10 Minutes

Cooking:
6 Minutes

Servings:
4

Ingredients
- 1 tbsp. black pepper
- 1 tbsp. dried oregano
- 1 tbsp. minced garlic
- 2 tbsp. lemon juice
- 2 tsp. olive oil
- 2 tsp. seal salt
- 8 pieces of lamb loin chops, around 4 ounces

Directions
1. In a big bowl or dish, combine the black pepper, salt, minced garlic, lemon juice, and oregano. Then rub it equally on all sides of the lamb chops.
2. Then place a skillet on high heat. After a minute, coat skillet with the cooking spray and place the lamb chops in the skillet. Sear chops for a minute on each side.
3. Lower heat to medium; continue cooking chops for 2-3 minutes per side until the desired doneness is reached.
4. Let the chops rest for five minutes before serving.

Nutritions: Calories 457: Protein 63g: Fat 9g: Carbs 4g

Asian Beef Short Ribs

Preparation:
15 Minutes

Cooking:
12 Hours

Servings:
4

Directions

1. Place all ingredients except for the sesame oil in the instant pot.
2. Close the lid and make sure that the steam release valve is set to "Venting".
3. Press the "slow cook" button and adjust the cooking time to 12 hours.
4. Once cooked, remove from pot and place into serving dishes. Drizzle with sesame oil, serve.

Ingredients

- 2 pounds beef short ribs
- 1 cup water
- 1 onion, sliced
- 1 tbsp. Szechuan peppercorns
- 2 tbsp. curry powder
- 3 tbsp. coconut amino
- 6 pieces star anise
- 6 tbsp. sesame oil
- Salt and pepper to taste

Nutritions: *Calories 592: Protein 47 g: Fat 44g: Carbs 6g*

Buffalo Turkey Balls

Preparation:
10 Minutes

Cooking:
40 Minutes

Servings:
5

Ingredients

- 2 eggs
- 1 pound ground turkey
- 1/2 cup hot sauce
- 1/2 stick unsalted butter
- 1/4 cup almond flour
- 3 tbsp. blue cheese, crumbled
- 2 oz. whipped cream cheese

Directions

1. Preheat oven to 350°F.
2. Mix the turkey meat, cream cheese, egg, blue cheese, and almond flour in a mixing bowl. Mix well and evenly divide into 20 small meatballs.
3. Place the meatballs on a greased baking pan.
4. Bake for 15 minutes.
5. While the meatballs are cooking, make the sauce by mixing the butter and hot sauce in a small saucepan.
6. Remove the meatballs from the oven and dip them in the hot sauce.
7. Place the meatballs in the oven and re-bake for another 15 minutes.
8. Remove the meatballs from the oven and place them into serving dishes. Garnish with chopped scallions or parsley.

Nutritions: Calories 300: Protein 30g: Fat 18g: Carbs 2g

Coconut Chicken

Preparation:
15 Minutes

Cooking:
25 Minutes

Servings:
4

Ingredients

- 2 tablespoons olive oil
- 4 (4 oz.) chicken breasts, cut into 2-inch chunks
- 1/2 cup chopped sweet onion
- 1 cup coconut milk   1 tablespoon curry powder
- 1 teaspoon ground cumin
- 1 teaspoon ground coriander
- 1/4 cup chopped fresh cilantro

Directions

1. Place a large saucepan over medium-high heat and add the olive oil.
2. Sauté the chicken until almost cooked through, about 10 minutes.
3. Add the onion and sauté for an additional 3 minutes.
4. In a medium bowl, whisk together the coconut milk; curry powder cumin, and coriander.
5. Pour the sauce into the saucepan with the chicken and bring the liquid to a boil.
6. Reduce the heat and simmer until the chicken is tender and the sauce has thickened, about 10 minutes.
7. Serve the chicken with the sauce, topped with cilantro.

Nutritions: Calories 382: Fat 31g: Protein 23g: Carbs 5g

Buffalo Drumsticks with Chili Aioli

Preparation:
15 Minutes

Cooking:
40 Minutes

Servings:
4

Ingredients

- 2 lbs. chicken drumsticks or chicken wings
- 2 tbsp. olive oil or coconut oil
- 2 tbsp. white wine vinegar
- 1 tbsp. tomato paste
- 1 tbsp. salt
- 1 tsp. paprika powder
- 1 tbsp. Tabasco
- Butter or olive oil for greasing the baking dish
- Chili aioli
- 2/3 cup mayonnaise
- 1 tbsp. smoked paprika powder or smoked chili powder
- 1 garlic clove, minced

Directions

1. Preheat oven to 450°F.
2. Put the drumsticks in a plastic bag.
3. Mix the ingredients for the marinade in a small bowl and pour it into the plastic bag. Shake the bag thoroughly and let marinate for 10 minutes at room temperature.
4. Coat a baking dish with oil. Place the drumsticks in the baking dish and let bake for 30-40 minutes or until they are done and have turned a nice color.
5. Mix together mayonnaise, garlic, and chili.
6. Serve warm

Nutritions: Calories 330: Fat 56g: Protein 42g: Carbs 2g

Cucumber Avocado Salad with Bacon

Preparation:
10 Minutes

Cooking:
-

Servings:
2

Ingredients
- 2 cups fresh baby spinach, chopped
- 1/2 English cucumber, sliced thin
- 1 small avocado, pitted and chopped
- 1 1/2 tablespoon olive oil
- 1 1/2 tablespoon lemon juice
- Salt and pepper
- 2 slices cooked bacon, chopped

Directions
1. Combine the spinach, cucumber, and avocado in a salad bowl. Toss with olive oil, lemon juice, salt, and pepper. Top with chopped bacon to serve.

Nutritions: *Calories: 365, Fat: 24.5g, Protein: 7g, Carbs: 13g, Fiber: 8g*

Bacon Cheeseburger Soup

Preparation:
10 Minutes

Cooking:
15 Minutes

Servings:
4

Ingredients

- 4 slices uncooked bacon
- 8 ounces ground beef (80% lean)
- 1 medium yellow onion, chopped
- 1 clove garlic, minced
- 3 cups beef broth
- 2 tablespoons tomato paste
- 2 teaspoons Dijon mustard
- Salt and pepper
- 1 cup shredded lettuce
- 1/2 cup shredded cheddar cheese

Directions

1. Cook the bacon in a saucepan until crisp then drain on paper towels and chop.
2. Reheat the bacon fat in the saucepan and add the beef.
3. Cook until the beef is browned then drains away half the fat.
4. Reheat the saucepan and add the onion and garlic – cook for 6 minutes.
5. Stir in the broth, tomato paste, and mustard then season with salt and pepper.
6. Add the beef and simmer on medium-low for 15 minutes, covered.
7. Spoon into bowls and top with shredded lettuce, cheddar cheese, and bacon.

Nutritions: Calories: 315; Fat: 20g; Protein: 27g; Carbs: 6g; Fiber: 1g

Egg Salad over Lettuce

Preparation:
10 Minutes

Cooking:
-

Servings:
2

Directions
1. Peel and dice the eggs into a mixing bowl.
2. Stir in the celery, mayonnaise, parsley, lemon juice, salt, and pepper.
3. Serve spooned over fresh chopped lettuce.

Ingredients
- 3 large hardboiled eggs, cooled
- 1 small stalk celery, diced
- 3 tablespoons mayonnaise
- 1 tablespoon fresh chopped parsley
- 1 teaspoon fresh lemon juice
- Salt and pepper
- 4 cups fresh chopped lettuce

Nutritions: Calories: 260, Fat: 23g, Protein: 10g, Carbs: 4g, Fiber: 1g

Egg Drop Soup

Preparation:
5 Minutes

Cooking:
10 Minutes

Servings:
4

Directions

1. Crush the bouillon cubes and stir into the broth in a saucepan.
2. Bring it to a boil, and then stir in the chili garlic paste.
3. Cook until steaming, and then remove from heat.
4. While whisking, drizzle in the beaten eggs.
5. Let sit for 2 minutes then serve with sliced green onion.

Ingredients

- 5 cups chicken broth
- 4 chicken bouillon cubes
- 1 1/2 tablespoons chili garlic paste
- 6 large eggs, whisked
- 1/2 green onion, sliced

Nutritions: Calories: 165, Fat: 9.5g, Protein: 16g, Carbs: 2.5g, Fiber: 0.5g

Spinach Cauliflower Soup

Preparation:
5 Minutes

Cooking:
15 Minutes

Servings:
4

Ingredients

- 1 tablespoon coconut oil
- 1 small yellow onion, chopped
- 2 cloves garlic, minced
- 2 cups chopped cauliflower
- 8 ounces fresh baby spinach, chopped
- 3 cups vegetable broth
- 1/2 cup canned coconut milk
- Salt and pepper

Directions

1. Heat the oil in a saucepan over medium-high heat – add the onion and garlic.
2. Sauté for 4 to 5 minutes until browned, then stir in the cauliflower.
3. Cook for 5 minutes until browned, and then stir in the spinach.
4. Let it cook for 2 minutes until wilted, then stir in the broth and bring to boil.
5. Remove from heat and puree the soup with an immersion blender.
6. Stir in the coconut milk and season with salt and pepper to taste. Serve hot.

Nutritions: Calories: 165, Fat: 12g, Protein: 7g, Carbs: 9g, Fiber: 2.5g

Easy Chopped Salad

Preparation:
15 Minutes

Cooking:
-

Servings:
2

Directions
1. Divide the lettuce between two salad plates or bowls.
2. Top the salads with diced avocado, tomato, and celery.
3. Add the sliced egg, diced ham, and shredded cheese.
4. Serve the salads with your favorite Keto-friendly dressing.

Ingredients
- 4 cups fresh chopped lettuce
- 1 small avocado, pitted and chopped
- 1/2 cup cherry tomatoes, halved
- 1/4 cup diced cucumber
- 2 hardboiled eggs, peeled and sliced
- 1 cup diced ham
- 1/2 cup shredded cheddar cheese

Nutritions: Calories: 520, Fat: 39.5g, Protein: 27g, Carbs: 17.5g, Fiber: 9g

Three Meat and Cheese Sandwich

Preparation:
30 Minutes

Cooking:
5 Minutes

Servings:
1

Ingredients

- 1 large egg, separated
- Pinch cream of tartar
- Pinch salt
- 1 ounce cream cheese, softened
- 1 ounce sliced ham
- 1 ounce sliced hard salami
- 1 ounce sliced turkey
- 2 slices cheddar cheese

Directions

1. For the bread, preheat the oven to 305°F and line a baking sheet with parchment.
2. Beat the egg whites with the cream of tartar and salt until soft peaks form.
3. Whisk the cream cheese and egg yolk until smooth and pale yellow.
4. Fold in the egg whites a little at a time until it is smooth and well combined.
5. Spoon the batter onto the baking sheet into two even circles.
6. Bake for 25 minutes until firm and lightly browned.
7. To complete the sandwich, layer the sliced meats and cheeses between the two bread circles.
8. Grease a skillet with cooking spray and heat over medium heat.
9. Add the sandwich and cook until browned underneath then flip and cook until the cheese is melted.

Nutritions: Calories: 610; Fat: 48g; Protein: 40g; Carbs: 3g; Fiber: 0.5g

Beef and Pepper Kebabs

Preparation:
30 Minutes

Cooking:
10 Minutes

Servings:
2

Directions

1. Whisk together the olive oil, balsamic vinegar, and mustard in a shallow dish.
2. Season the steak with salt and pepper, then toss in the marinade.
3. Let marinate for 30 minutes, and then slide onto skewers with the peppers.
4. Preheat a grill pan to high heat and grease with cooking spray.
5. Cook the kebabs for 2 to 3 minutes on each side until the beef is done.

Ingredients

- 2 tablespoons olive oil
- 1 1/2 tablespoon balsamic vinegar
- 2 teaspoons Dijon mustard
- Salt and pepper
- 8 ounces beef sirloin, cut into 2-inch pieces
- 1 small red pepper, cut into chunks
- 1 small green pepper, cut into chunks

Nutritions: Calories: 365, Fat: 21.5g, Protein: 35.5g, Carbs: 6.5g, Fiber: 1.5g

Slow-Cooker Chicken Fajita Soup

Preparation:
10 Minutes

Cooking:
6 Hours

Servings:
4

Ingredients

- 12 ounces chicken thighs
- 1 cup diced tomatoes
- 2 cups chicken stock
- 1/2 cup enchilada sauce
- 2 ounces chopped green chiles
- 1 tablespoon minced garlic
- 1 medium yellow onion, chopped
- 1 small red pepper, chopped
- 1 jalapeno, seeded and minced
- 2 teaspoons chili powder
- ¾ teaspoon paprika
- 1/2 teaspoon ground cumin
- Salt and pepper
- 1 small avocado, sliced thinly
- 1/4 cup chopped cilantro
- 1 lime, cut into wedges

Directions

1. Combine the chicken, tomatoes, chicken stock, enchilada sauce, chiles, and garlic in the slow cooker and stir well.
2. Add the onion, bell peppers, and jalapeno.
3. Stir in the seasonings, then cover and cook on low for 5 to 6 hours.
4. Remove the chicken and chop or shred then stir it back into the soup.
5. Spoon into bowls and serve with sliced avocado, cilantro, and lime wedges.

Nutritions: *Calories: 325, Fat: 17g, Protein: 28g, Carbs: 17g, Fiber: 7g*

Avocado Egg Salad on Lettuce

Preparation:
10 Minutes

Cooking:
-

Servings:
2

Directions

1. Coarsely chop the eggs into a bowl.
2. Toss in the avocado, celery, red onion, and lemon juice.
3. Season with salt and pepper then serve over chopped lettuce.

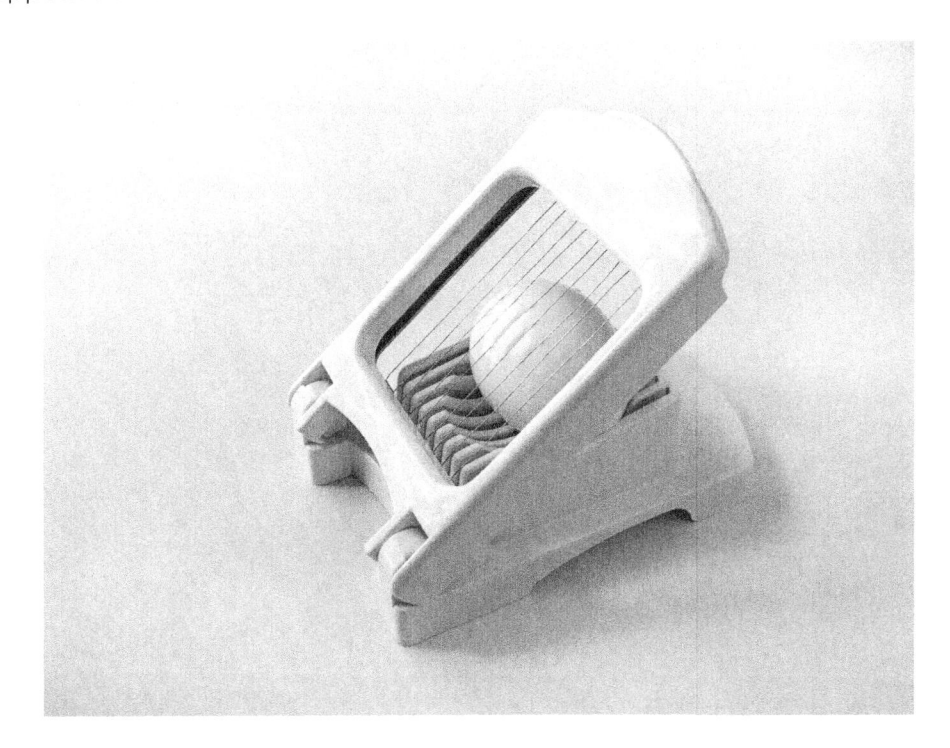

Ingredients

- 4 large hardboiled eggs, cooled and peeled
- 1 small avocado, pitted and chopped
- 1 medium stalk celery, diced
- 1/4 cup diced red onion
- 2 tablespoons fresh lemon juice
- Salt and pepper
- 4 cups chopped romaine lettuce

Nutritions: Calories: 375, Fat: 30g, Protein: 15.5g, Carbs: 15g, Fiber: 8g

Mediterranean Keto Dish

Preparation:
5 Minutes

Cooking:
-

Servings:
2

Directions
1. Take two Serves plates and then distribute tomato, cheese, and tuna evenly between them.
2. Season with salt and black pepper and then serve with olive oil.

Ingredients
- 1 Roma tomato, halved
- 1/4 cup olive oil
- 2 ounces fresh mozzarella cheese, sliced
- 2 ounces tuna, packed in water
- 8 green olives

Nutritions: Calories: 412, Fat: 35g, Protein: 20g, Carbs: 4g, Fiber: 1.5g

Easy Zucchini Noodles

Preparation:
5 Minutes

Cooking:
10 Minutes

Servings:
2

Ingredients

- 1 large zucchini, spiralized into noodles
- 2 tablespoons softened cream cheese
- 1 tablespoon grated parmesan cheese
- 1/8 teaspoon garlic powder

Directions

1. Prepare zucchini noodles, and for this, cut zucchini into noodles by using a spiralizer or a vegetable peeler.
2. Then bring out a skillet pan, place it over medium-high heat, add zucchini noodles and garlic, toss well until mixed, and cook for 4 minutes until slightly soft.
3. Push noodles to one side of the pan, add cream cheese into the other side of the pan, stir it until melts, then mix with noodles until coated and season with salt and black pepper.
4. Remove pan from heat, sprinkle noodles with parmesan cheese and serve.

Nutritions: *Calories: 107, Fat: 9g, Protein: 2g, Carbs: 2g, Fiber: 1g*

Keto Cheese Potato

Preparation:
5 Minutes

Cooking:
15 Minutes

Servings:
2

Ingredients
- 1 large turnip, peeled, diced
- 2 slices of bacon, chopped
- 1 tablespoon olive oil
- 1 tablespoon softened cream cheese
- 1/4 of spring onion, diced, and more for garnishing

Directions
1. Bring out a skillet pan, place it over medium-high heat, add oil and when hot, add diced turnip, season with salt, black pepper, and paprika, sprinkle with garlic, stir well and cook for 5 minutes.
2. Then add onion, stir and continue cooking for 3 minutes until onions start to soften.
3. Add chopped bacon, continue cooking for 5 to 7 minutes, or until bacon is crispy and remove the pan from heat.
4. Top with green onions and cream cheese and then serve.

Nutritions: Calories: 88, Fat: 9g, Protein: 3g, Carbs: 3.5g, Fiber: 1g

CHAPTER 10.
Dinner Recipes

Grilled Pesto Salmon with Asparagus

Preparation:
5 Minutes

Cooking:
15 Minutes

Servings:
5

Directions
1. Preheat the grill to heat, and oil the grills.
2. Season the salmon with salt and pepper and sprinkle with spray to cook.
3. Grill the salmon on each side for 4 to 5 minutes, until cooked.
4. Throw the asparagus with oil and grill for about 10 minutes, until tender.
5. Spoon the salmon with the pesto, and serve with the asparagus.

Ingredients
- 4 (6-ounce) boneless salmon fillets
- Salt and pepper
- 1 bunch asparagus, ends trimmed
- 2 tablespoons olive oil
- 1/4 cup basil pesto

Nutritions: 300 calories, 17.5 g of fat, 34.5 g of protein, 2.5 g of carbohydrates, 1.5 g of fiber, 1 g of net carbs

Cheddar-Stuffed Burgers with Zucchini

Preparation:
10 Minutes

Cooking:
15 Minutes

Servings:
4

Ingredients

- 1 pound ground beef (80% lean)
- 2 large eggs
- 1/4 cup almond flour
- 1 cup shredded cheddar cheese
- Salt and pepper
- 2 tablespoons olive oil
- 1 large zucchini, halved and sliced

Directions

1. In a cup, add the beef, egg, almond flour, cheese, salt, and pepper.
2. Mix well, then shape into 4 even-sized patties.
3. Heat up the oil over medium to high heat in a large skillet.
4. Add the burger patties, and cook until browned for 5 minutes.
5. Flip the patties onto the skillet and add the zucchini, tossing to cover with grease.
6. Add salt and pepper and boil for 5 minutes, stirring the mixture.

Nutritions: 440 calories, 27.5 g of fat, 45 g of protein, 8 g of carbohydrates, 2.5 g of fiber, 4.5 g of net carbs

Chicken Cordon Bleu with Cauliflower

Preparation:
10 Minutes

Cooking:
45 Minutes

Servings:
4

Ingredients

- 4 boneless chicken breast halves (about 12 ounces)
- 4 slices deli ham
- 4 slices Swiss cheese
- 1 large egg, whisked well
- 2 ounces pork rinds
- 1/4 cup almond flour
- 1/4 cup grated parmesan cheese
- 1/2 teaspoon garlic powder
- Salt and pepper
- 2 cups cauliflower florets

Directions

1. Preheat the oven to 350 ° F and add a foil on a baking sheet.
2. Sandwich the breast half of the chicken between parchment parts and pound flat.
3. Spread the bits out and cover with ham and cheese sliced over.
4. Roll the chicken over the fillings and then dip into the beaten egg.
5. In a food processor, mix the pork rinds, almond flour, parmesan, garlic powder, salt and pepper, and pulse into fine crumbs.
6. Roll the rolls of chicken in the mixture of pork rind then put them on the baking sheet.
7. Throw the cauliflower into the baking sheet with the melted butter and fold.
8. Bake for 45 minutes until the chicken is fully cooked.

Nutritions: Calories 420, Fat 23.5 g, Protein 45 g, Carbohydrates 7 g, Fiber 2.5 g, Net Carbs 4.5 g

Sesame-Crusted Tuna with Green Beans

Preparation:
15 Minutes

Cooking:
5 Minutes

Servings:
4

Ingredients

- 1/4 cup white sesame seeds
- 1/4 cup black sesame seeds
- 4 (6-ounce) ahi tuna steaks
- Salt and pepper
- 1 tablespoon olive oil
- 1 tablespoon coconut oil
- 2 cups green beans

Directions

1. In a shallow dish, mix the two kinds of sesame seeds.
2. Season the tuna with pepper and salt.
3. Dredge the tuna in a mixture of sesame seeds.
4. Heat up to high heat the olive oil in a skillet, then add the tuna.
5. Cook for 1 to 2 minutes until it turns seared, then sear on the other side.
6. Remove the tuna from the skillet, and let the tuna rest while using the coconut oil to heat the skillet.
7. Fry the green beans in the oil for 5 minutes then use sliced tuna to eat.

Nutritions: *380 calories, 19 g fat, 44.5 g protein, 8 g carbs, 3 g fiber, 5 g net carbs*

Rosemary Roasted Cauliflower

Preparation: 10 Minutes

Cooking: 20 Minutes

Servings: 4

Ingredients

- 1 1/2 pounds boneless pork tenderloin
- 1 tablespoon coconut oil
- 1 tablespoon fresh chopped rosemary
- Salt and pepper
- 1 tablespoon olive oil
- 2 cups cauliflower florets

Directions

1. Rub the coconut oil into the pork, then season with the rosemary, salt, and pepper.
2. Heat up the olive oil over medium to high heat in a large skillet.
3. Add the pork on each side and cook until browned for 2 to 3 minutes.
4. Sprinkle the cauliflower over the pork in the skillet.
5. Reduce heat to low, then cover the skillet and cook until the pork is cooked through for 8 to 10 minutes.
6. Slice the pork with cauliflower and eat.

Nutritions: 300 calories, 15.5 g of fat, 37 g of protein, 3 g of carbohydrates, 1.5 g of fiber, 1.5 g of net carbs

Chicken Tikka with Cauliflower Rice

Preparation:
10 Minutes

Cooking:
6 Hours

Servings:
6

Directions

1. Place the chicken in a slow cooker and then stir in the remaining ingredients, except for the butter and cauliflower.
2. Cover and cook for 6 hours on low heat until the chicken is cooked and the sauce is thickened.
3. Melt the butter over medium to high heat into a saucepan.
4. Remove the riced cauliflower, and cook until tender for 6 to 8 minutes.
5. Serve cauliflower rice with chicken tikka.

Ingredients

- 2 pounds boneless chicken thighs, chopped
- 1 cup canned coconut milk
- 1 cup heavy cream
- 3 tablespoons tomato paste
- 2 tablespoons garam masala
- 1 tablespoon fresh grated ginger
- 1 tablespoon minced garlic
- 1 tablespoon smoked paprika
- 2 teaspoons onion powder
- 1 teaspoon guar gum
- 1 tablespoon butter
- 1 1/2 cup rice cauliflower

Nutritions: 485 calories, 32 g of fat, 43 g of protein, 6.5 g of carbohydrates, 1.5 g of fiber, 5 g of net carbs

Grilled Salmon and Mango Sauce

Preparation:
5 Minutes

Cooking:
10 Minutes

Servings:
4

Ingredients
- 4 (6-ounce) boneless salmon fillets
- 1 tablespoon olive oil
- Salt and pepper
- 1 large zucchini, sliced into coins
- 2 tablespoons fresh lemon juice
- 1/2 cup chopped mango
- 1/4 cup fresh chopped cilantro
- 1 teaspoon lemon zest
- 1/2 cup canned coconut milk

Directions
1. Preheat a grill pan to heat, and sprinkle with cooking spray liberally.
2. Brush with olive oil to the salmon and season with salt and pepper.
3. Apply lemon juice to the zucchini, and season with salt and pepper.
4. Put the zucchini and salmon fillets on the grill pan.
5. Cook for 5 minutes then turn all over and cook for another 5 minutes.
6. Combine the remaining ingredients in a blender and combine to create a sauce.
7. Serve the side-drizzled salmon filets with mango sauce and zucchini.

Nutritions: *350 calories, 21.5 g of fat, 35 g of protein, 8 g of carbohydrates, 2 g of sugar, 6 g of net carbs*

Slow-Cooker Pot Roast with Green Beans

Preparation:
10 Minutes

Cooking:
8 Hours

Servings:
8

Ingredients

- 2 medium stalks celery, sliced
- 1 medium yellow onion, chopped
- 1 (3-pound) boneless beef chuck roast
- Salt and pepper
- 1/4 cup beef broth
- 2 tablespoons Worcestershire sauce
- 4 cups green beans, trimmed
- 2 tablespoons cold butter, chopped

Directions

1. In a slow-cooking dish, add the celery and onion.
2. Put the frying pan on top and season with salt and pepper.
3. Whisk the beef broth and Worcestershire sauce together then pour in.
4. Cover and cook for 8 hours on low heat, until the beef is very tender.
5. Bring the beef off on a cutting board and cut into chunks.
6. Return the beef to the slow cooker and add the chopped butter and the beans.
7. Cover and cook for 20 to 30 minutes on warm, until the beans are tender.

Nutritions: *375 calories, 13.5 g of fat, 53 g of protein, 6 g of carbohydrates, 2 g of fiber, 4 g of net carbs*

Beef and Broccoli Stir-Fry

Preparation:
20 Minutes

Cooking:
15 Minutes

Servings:
4

Ingredients

- 1/4 cup soy sauce
- 1 tablespoon sesame oil
- 1 teaspoon garlic chili paste
- 1 pound beef sirloin
- 2 tablespoons almond flour
- 2 tablespoons coconut oil
- 2 cups chopped broccoli florets
- 1 tablespoon grated ginger
- 3 cloves garlic, minced

Directions

1. In a small bowl, whisk the soy sauce, sesame oil, and chili paste together.
2. In a plastic freezer bag, slice the beef and mix with the almond flour.
3. Pour in the sauce and toss to coat for 20 minutes, then let rest.
4. Heat up the oil over medium to high heat in a large skillet.
5. In the pan, add the beef and sauce and cook until the beef is browned.
6. Move the beef to the skillet sides, and then add the broccoli, ginger, and garlic.
7. Sauté until tender-crisp broccoli, then throw it all together and serve hot.

Nutritions: *350 calories, 19 g fat, 37.5 g protein, 6.5 g carbs, 2 g fiber, 4.5 g net carbs*

Parmesan-Crusted Halibut with Asparagus

Preparation:
10 Minutes

Cooking:
15 Minutes

Servings:
4

Directions

1. Preheat the oven to 400 F and line a foil-based baking sheet.
2. Throw the asparagus in olive oil and scatter over the baking sheet.
3. In a blender, add the butter, Parmesan cheese, almond flour, garlic powder, salt and pepper, and mix until smooth.
4. Place the fillets with the asparagus on the baking sheet, and spoon the Parmesan over the fillets.
5. Bake for 10 to 12 minutes, and then broil until browned for 2 to 3 minutes.

Ingredients

- 2 tablespoons olive oil
- 1/4 cup butter, softened
- Salt and pepper
- 1/4 cup grated Parmesan
- 1 pound asparagus, trimmed
- 2 tablespoons almond flour
- 4 (6-ounce) boneless halibut fillets
- 1 teaspoon garlic powder

Nutritions: 415 calories, 26 g of fat, 42 g of protein, 6 g of carbohydrates, 3 g of fiber, 3 g of net carbs

Hearty Beef and Bacon Casserole

Preparation:
25 Minutes

Cooking:
30 Minutes

Servings:
8

Ingredients

- 8 slices uncooked bacon
- 1 medium head cauliflower, chopped
- 1/4 cup canned coconut milk
- Salt and pepper
- 2 pounds ground beef (80% lean)
- 8 ounces mushrooms, sliced
- 1 large yellow onion, chopped
- 2 cloves garlic, minced

Directions

1. Preheat to 375 F on the oven.
2. Cook the bacon in a skillet until it crispness, then drain and chop on paper towels.
3. Bring to boil a pot of salted water, and then add the cauliflower.
4. Boil until tender for 6 to 8 minutes then drain and add the coconut milk to a food processor.
5. Mix until smooth, then sprinkle with salt and pepper.
6. Cook the beef until browned in a pan, and then wash the fat away.
7. Remove the mushrooms, onion, and garlic, and then move to a baking platter.
8. Place on top of the cauliflower mixture and bake for 30 minutes.
9. Broil for 5 minutes on high heat, then sprinkle with bacon to serve.

Nutritions: 410 calories, 25.5 g of fat, 37 g of protein, 7.5 g of carbohydrates, 3 g of fiber, 4.5 g of net carbs

Sesame Wings with Cauliflower

Preparation:
5 Minutes

Cooking:
30 Minutes

Servings:
4

Directions

1. In a freezer bag, mix the soy sauce, sesame oil, balsamic vinegar, garlic, ginger, and salt, then add the chicken wings.
2. Coat flip, and then chill for 2 to 3 hours.
3. Preheat the oven to 400 F and line a foil-based baking sheet.
4. Spread the wings along with the cauliflower onto the baking sheet.
5. Bake for 35 minutes, and then sprinkle on to serve with sesame seeds.

Ingredients

- 2 1/2 tablespoons soy sauce
- 2 tablespoons sesame oil
- 1 1/2 teaspoons balsamic vinegar
- 1 teaspoon minced garlic
- 1 teaspoon grated ginger
- Salt
- 1 pound chicken wing, the wings itself
- 2 cups cauliflower florets

Nutritions: *400 calories, 28.5 g of fat, 31.5 g of protein, 4 g of carbohydrates, 1.5 g of fiber, 2.5 g of carbs*

Chicken Pan with Veggies and Pesto

Preparation:
10 Minutes

Cooking:
20 Minutes

Servings:
4

Ingredients

- 2 Tbsp. olive oil
- 1 pound chicken thighs, boneless, skinless, sliced into strips
- ¾ cup oil-packed sun-dried tomatoes, chopped
- 1 pound asparagus ends
- 1/4 cup basil pesto
- 1 cup cherry tomatoes, red and yellow, halved
- Salt, to taste

Directions

1. Heat olive oil in a frying pan over medium-high heat.
2. Put salt on the chicken slices and then put into a skillet add the sun-dried tomatoes and fry for 5-10 minutes. Remove the chicken slices and season with salt. Add asparagus to the skillet. Cook for additional 5-10 minutes.
3. Place the chicken back in the skillet, pour in the pesto and whisk. Fry for 1-2 minutes. Remove from the heat. Add the halved cherry tomatoes and pesto. Stir well and serve.

Nutritions: *Carbohydrates 12 g, Fat 32 g, Protein 2 g, Calories 423*

Cabbage Soup with Beef

Preparation:
15 Minutes

Cooking:
20 Minutes

Servings:
4

Ingredients

- 2 Tbsp. olive oil
- 1 medium onion, chopped
- 1 pound fillet steak, cut into pieces
- 1/2 stalk celery, chopped
- 1 carrot, peeled and diced
- 1/2 head small green cabbage, cut into pieces
- 2 cloves garlic, minced
- 4 cups beef broth
- 2 Tbsp. fresh parsley, chopped
- 1 tsp. dried thyme
- 1 tsp. dried rosemary
- 1 tsp. garlic powder
- Salt and black pepper, to taste

Directions

1. Heat oil in a pot (use medium heat). Add the beef and cook until it is browned. Put the onion into the pot and boil for 3-4 minutes.
2. Add the celery and carrot. Stir well and cook for about 3-4 minutes. Add the cabbage and boil until it starts softening. Add garlic and simmer for about 1 minute.
3. Pour the broth into the pot. Add the parsley and garlic powder. Mix thoroughly and reduce heat to medium-low.
4. Cook for 10-15 minutes.

Nutritions: *Carbohydrates 4 g; Fat 11 g; Protein 12 g; Calories 177*

Cauliflower Rice Soup with Chicken

Preparation:
10 Minutes

Cooking:
1 Hour

Servings:
5

Directions

1. Put shredded chicken breasts into a saucepan and pour in the chicken broth. Add salt and pepper. Cook for 1 hour.
2. In another pot, melt the butter. Add the onion, garlic, and celery. Sauté until the mix is translucent. Add the rice cauliflower, rosemary, and carrot. Mix and cook for 7 minutes.
3. Add the chicken breasts and broth to the cauliflower mix. Put the lid on and simmer for 15 minutes.

Ingredients

- 2 1/2 pounds chicken breasts, boneless and skinless
- 8 Tbsp. butter
- 1/4 cup celery, chopped
- 1/2 cup onion, chopped
- 4 cloves garlic, minced
- 2 12-ounce packages steamed cauliflower rice
- 1 Tbsp. parsley, chopped
- 2 tsp. poultry seasoning
- 1/2 cup carrot, grated
- 3/4 tsp. rosemary
- 1 tsp. salt
- 3/4 tsp. pepper
- 4 ounces cream cheese
- 4 3/4 cup chicken broth

Nutritions: Carbohydrates 6g; Fat 30g; Protein 27g; Calories 415

Quick Pumpkin Soup

Preparation:
10 Minutes

Cooking:
20 Minutes

Servings:
4-6

Directions

1. Combine the coconut milk, broth, baked pumpkin, and spices in a soup pan (use medium heat). Stir occasionally and simmer for 15 minutes.
2. With an immersion blender, blend the soup mix for 1 minute.
3. Top with sour cream or coconut yogurt and pumpkin seeds.

Ingredients

- 1 cup coconut milk
- 2 cups chicken broth
- 6 cups baked pumpkin
- 1 tsp. garlic powder
- 1 tsp. ground cinnamon
- 1 tsp. dried ginger
- 1 tsp. nutmeg
- 1 tsp. paprika
- Salt and pepper, to taste
- Sour cream or coconut yogurt, for topping
- Pumpkin seeds, toasted, for topping

Nutritions: Carbohydrates 8.1 g, Fat 9.8 g, Protein 3.1 g, Calories 123

Fresh Avocado Soup

Preparation:
5 Minutes

Cooking:
10 Minutes

Servings:
2

Directions
1. Mix all your ingredients thoroughly in a blender.
2. Chill in the fridge for 5-10 minutes.

Ingredients
- 1 ripe avocado
- 2 romaine lettuce leaves, washed and chopped
- 1 cup coconut milk, chilled
- 1 Tbsp. lime juice
- 20 fresh mint leaves
- Salt, to taste

Nutritions: *Carbohydrates 12 g, Fat 26 g, Protein 4 g, Calories 280*

Creamy Garlic Chicken

Preparation:
5 Minutes

Cooking:
15 Minutes

Servings:
4

Ingredients

- 4 chicken breasts, finely sliced
- 1 tsp. garlic powder
- 1 tsp. paprika
- 2 Tbsp. butter
- 1 tsp. salt
- 1 cup heavy cream
- 1/2 cup sun-dried tomatoes
- 2 cloves garlic, minced
- 1 cup spinach, chopped

Directions

1. Blend the paprika, garlic powder, and salt and sprinkle over both sides of the chicken.
2. Melt the butter in a frying pan (choose medium heat). Add the chicken breast and fry for 5 minutes on each side. Set aside.
3. Add the heavy cream, sun-dried tomatoes, and garlic to the pan and whisk well to combine. Cook for 2 minutes. Add spinach and sauté for an additional 3 minutes. Return the chicken to the pan and cover with the sauce.

Nutritions: Carbohydrates 12 g, Fat 26 g, Protein 4 g, Calories 280

Cauliflower Cheesecake

Preparation:
20 Minutes

Cooking:
30 Minutes

Servings:
6

Directions

1. Preheat the oven to 350°F.
2. Boil the cauliflower florets for 5 minutes.
3. In a separate bowl combine the cream cheese and sour cream. Mix well and add the cheddar cheese, bacon pieces, green onion, salt, pepper, and garlic powder. Put the cauliflower florets into the bowl and combine with the sauce.
4. Put the cauliflower mix on the baking tray and bake for 15-20 minutes.

Ingredients

- 1 head cauliflower, cut into florets
- 1/3 cup sour cream
- 4 oz. cream cheese, softened
- 1 1/2 cup cheddar cheese, shredded
- 6 pieces bacon, cooked and chopped
- 1 tsp. salt
- 1/2 tsp. black pepper
- 1/4 cup green onion, chopped
- 1/4 tsp. garlic powder

Nutritions: *Carbohydrates 8 g, Fat 26 g, Protein 15 g, Calories 320*

Chinese Pork Bowl

Preparation:
5 Minutes

Cooking:
15 Minutes

Servings:
4

Directions

1. Fry the pork over medium-high heat until it is starting to turn golden brown.
2. Combine the garlic cloves, butter, and Brussels sprouts. Add to the pan, whisk well and cook until the sprouts turn golden brown.
3. Stir the soy sauce and rice vinegar together and pour the sauce into the pan.
4. Sprinkle with salt and pepper.
5. Top with chopped leek.

Ingredients

- 1 1/4 pounds pork belly, cut into bite-size pieces
- 2 Tbsp. tamari soy sauce
- 1 Tbsp. rice vinegar
- 2 cloves garlic, smashed
- 3 oz. butter
- 1 pound Brussels sprouts, rinsed, trimmed, halved or quartered
- 1/2 leek, chopped
- Salt and ground black pepper, to taste

Nutritions: *Carbohydrates 7 g, Fat 97 g, Protein 19 g, Calories 993*

Turkey-Pepper Mix

Preparation:
20 Minutes

Cooking:
0 Minutes

Servings:
1

Ingredients

- 1 pound turkey tenderloin, cut into thin steaks
- 1 tsp. salt, divided
- 2 Tbsp. extra-virgin olive oil, divided
- 1/2 sweet onion, sliced
- 1 red bell pepper, cut into strips
- 1 yellow bell pepper, cut into strips
- 1/2 tsp. Italian seasoning
- 1/4 tsp. ground black pepper
- 2 tsp. red wine vinegar
- 1 14-ounces can crushed tomatoes, roasted
- Fresh parsley
- Basil

Directions

1. Sprinkle 1/2 tsp. salt on your turkey. Pour 1 Tbsp. oil into the pan and heat it. Add the turkey steaks and cook for 1-3 minutes per side. Set aside.
2. Put the onion, bell peppers, and the remaining salt in the pan and cook for 7 minutes, stirring all the time. Sprinkle with Italian seasoning and add black pepper. Cook for 30 seconds. Add the tomatoes and vinegar and fry the mix for about 20 seconds.
3. Return the turkey to the pan and pour the sauce over it. Simmer for 2-3 minutes.
4. Top with chopped parsley and basil.

Nutritions: *Carbohydrates 11 g, Fat 8 g, Protein 30 g, Calories 230*

Shrimp Scampi with Garlic

Preparation:
5 Minutes

Cooking:
10 Minutes

Servings:
4

Directions

1. Pour the olive oil into the previously heated frying pan. Add the garlic and shallots and fry for about 2 minutes.
2. Combine the Pinot Grigio, salted butter, and lemon juice. Pour this mix into the pan and cook for 5 minutes.
3. Put the parsley, black pepper, red pepper flakes, and sea salt into the pan and whisk well.
4. Add the shrimp and fry until they are pink (about 3 minutes).

Ingredients

- 1 pound shrimp
- 3 Tbsp. olive oil
- 1 bulb shallot, sliced
- 4 cloves garlic, minced
- 1/2 cup Pinot Grigio
- 4 Tbsp. salted butter
- 1 Tbsp. lemon juice
- 1/2 tsp. sea salt
- 1/4 tsp. black pepper
- 1/4 tsp. red pepper flakes
- 1/4 cup parsley, chopped

Nutritions: *Carbohydrates 7 g, Fat 7 g, Protein 32 g, Calories 344*

Cucumber Salad with Tomatoes and Feta

Preparation:
15 Minutes

Cooking:
0 Minutes

Servings:
4

Ingredients

- 2 cucumbers, diced
- 6 tomatoes, diced
- ¾ cup feta cheese, crumbled
- 1/2 white onion, chopped
- 1 clove garlic, minced
- 2 Tbsp. lime juice
- 2 Tbsp. parsley, chopped
- 2 Tbsp. dill, chopped
- 3 Tbsp. olive oil
- 3 Tbsp. red wine vinegar
- Salt and black pepper, to taste

Directions

1. Combine all the ingredients in a bowl.
2. Stir thoroughly and serve.

Nutritions: *Carbohydrates 5 g, Fat 10 g, Protein 3 g, Calories 125*

Crab Cakes with Almond Flour

Preparation:
1 Hour 15 Minutes

Cooking:
15 Minutes

Servings:
4

Directions

1. In a separate bowl, combine the crabmeat, garlic, parsley, egg, mayonnaise, mustard, kosher salt, thyme, cayenne pepper, and almond flour. Stir well. Form 4 cakes and place them into a fridge for 1 hour.
2. Melt the butter in the pan and put in your crab cakes. Fry for about 5-7 minutes on each side.

Ingredients

- 8 oz. fresh crab meat, shells removed
- 1 Tbsp. garlic, minced
- 1/4 cup parsley, chopped
- 1 egg, slightly beaten
- 1 tbsp. avocado oil mayonnaise
- 1 tbsp. mustard
- 1/2 tsp. kosher salt
- 1/2 tsp. dried thyme
- 1/8 tsp. cayenne pepper
- 1/2 cup almond flour
- 2 tbsp. butter, for frying

Nutritions: *Carbohydrates 4 g, Fat 17 g, Protein 13 g, Calories 219*

Stuffed Eggs with Bacon-Avocado Filling

Preparation:
10 Minutes

Cooking:
10 Minutes

Servings:
1

Directions

1. Fry the bacon for 3 minutes in a pan. Add the avocado and fry for an additional 3 minutes (lower heat).
2. Combine the mayonnaise, mustard, lemon, garlic powder, and salt in a separate bowl. Stir well.
3. Remove the yolk from the halved eggs and fill the egg halves with the mayonnaise mix. Top with the bacon-avocado filling.

Ingredients

- 2 eggs, boiled and halved
- 1 Tbsp. mayonnaise
- 1/4 tsp. mustard
- 1/8 lemon, squeezed
- 1/4 tsp. garlic powder
- 1/8 tsp. salt
- 1/8 tsp. smoked paprika
- 1/4 avocado
- 16 small pieces bacon

Nutritions: *Carbohydrates 4 g, Fat 30 g, Protein 16 g, Calories 342*

Simple Tuna Salad

Preparation:
5 Minutes

Cooking:
0 Minutes

Servings:
4

Ingredients

- 10 oz. canned tuna, drained
- 1 avocado, chopped
- 1 rib celery, chopped
- 2 cloves fresh garlic, minced
- 3 Tbsp. mayonnaise
- 1 red onion, chopped
- Tbsp. lemon juice
- 8 sprigs parsley
- 1/4 cucumber, chopped
- Salt and pepper, to taste

Directions

1. Divide the parsley into two halves.
2. Mix all the ingredients except half of the parsley in a separate bowl. Stir well.
3. Add salt and pepper to taste.
4. Top with the remaining parsley.

Nutritions: *Carbohydrates 1.7 g, Fat 16.3 g, Protein 13.9 g, Calories 225*

CHAPTER 11.
Snacks Recipes

Banana Waffles

Preparation:
30 Minutes

Cooking:
30 Minutes

Servings:
4

Directions

1. Mash the banana thoroughly until you get a mashed potato consistency.
2. Add all the other ingredients in and whisk thoroughly to evenly distribute the dry and wet ingredients. You should be able to get a pancake-like consistency
3. Fry the waffles in a pan or use a waffle maker.
4. You can serve it with hazelnut spread and fresh berries. Enjoy!

Ingredients

- 4 eggs
- 1 ripe banana
- ¾ cup coconut milk
- ¾ cup almond flour
- 1 pinch of salt
- 1 tbsp. of ground psyllium husk powder
- 1/2 tsp. vanilla extract
- 1 tsp. baking powder
- 1 tsp. of ground cinnamon
- Butter or coconut oil for frying

Nutritions: each waffle contains 4g of carbohydrates, 13g fat, 5g protein, and 155 calories

Keto Cinnamon Coffee

Preparation:
5 Minutes

Cooking:
5 Minutes

Servings:
1

Directions

1. Start by mixing the cinnamon with the ground coffee.
2. Pour in hot water and do what you usually do when brewing.
3. Use a mixer or whisk to whip the cream 'til you get stiff peaks
4. Serve in a tall mug and put the whipped cream on the surface. Sprinkle with some cinnamon and enjoy.

Ingredients

- 2 tbsp. ground coffee
- 1/3 cup heavy whipping cream
- 1 tsp. ground cinnamon
- 2 cups water

Nutritions: *Net Carbs 1g, Fiber 1g, Fat 14grs, Protein 1gr, Calories 136k*

Keto Waffles and Blueberries

Preparation:
15 Minutes

Cooking:
10-15 Minutes

Servings:
8

Directions

1. Start by mixing the butter and eggs first until you get a smooth batter. Put in the remaining ingredients except those that we'll be using as a topping.
2. Heat your waffle iron to medium temperature and start pouring in the batter for cooking
3. In a separate bowl, mix the butter and blueberries using a hand mixer. Use this to top off your freshly cooked waffles

Ingredients

- 8 eggs
- 5 oz. melted butter
- 1 tsp. vanilla extract
- 2 tsp. baking powder
- 1/3 cup coconut flour
- 3 oz. butter (topping)
- 1 oz. fresh blueberries (topping)

Nutritions: *Net Carbs 3g, Fiber 5g, Fat 56g, Protein 14g, Calories 575k*

Mushroom Omelet

Preparation:
15 Minutes

Cooking:
5 Minutes

Servings:
1

Ingredients

- 3 eggs, medium
- 1 oz. shredded cheese
- 1 oz. butter used for frying
- 1/4 yellow onion, chopped
- 4 large sliced mushrooms
- Your favorite vegetables, optional
- Salt and pepper to taste

Directions

1. Crack and whisk the eggs in a bowl. Add some salt and pepper to taste.
2. Melt the butter in a pan using low heat. Put in the mushroom and onion, cooking the two until you get that amazing smell.
3. Pour the egg mix into the pan and allow it to cook on medium heat.
4. Allow the bottom part to cook before sprinkling the cheese on top of the still-raw portion of the egg.
5. Carefully pry the edges of the omelet and fold it in half. Allow it to cook for a few more seconds before removing the pan from the heat and sliding it directly onto your plate.

Nutritions: *Carbohydrates 5g; Fiber 1g; Fat 44grs; Protein 26g; Calories 520k*

Chocolate Sea Salt Smoothie

Preparation:
15 Minutes

Cooking:
5 Minutes

Servings:
2

Directions
1. Combine all the ingredients in a high-speed blender and mix until you get a soft smoothie.
2. Add ice and enjoy!

Ingredients
- 1 avocado (frozen or not)
- 2 cups almond milk
- 1 tbsp tahini
- 1/4 cup cocoa powder
- 1 scoop perfect Keto chocolate base

Nutritions: Calories 235, Fat 20g, Carbohydrates 11.25, Fiber 8g, Protein 5.5g

Zucchini Lasagna

Preparation:
20 Minutes

Cooking:
1 Hour 20 Minutes

Servings:
9

Ingredients

- 3 cups raw macadamia nuts or soaked blanched almonds (for ricotta)
- 2 tbsp. nutritional yeast (for ricotta)
- 2 tsp. dried oregano (for ricotta)
- 1 tsp. sea salt (for ricotta)
- 1/2 cup water or more as needed (for ricotta)
- 1/4 cup vegan parmesan cheese (for ricotta)
- 1/2 cup fresh basil, chopped (for ricotta)
- 1 medium lemon, juiced (for ricotta)
- Black pepper to taste (for ricotta)
- 1 28-oz jar favorite marinara sauce
- 3 medium zucchini squash thinly sliced with a mandolin

Directions

1. Preheat the oven to 375 degrees Fahrenheit
2. Put macadamia nuts in a food processor.
3. Add the remaining ingredients and continue to puree the mixture. You want to create a fine paste.
4. Taste and adjust the seasonings depending on your personal preferences.
5. Pour 1 cup of marinara sauce into a baking dish.
6. Start creating the lasagna layers using thinly sliced zucchini
7. Scoop small amounts of the ricotta mixture on the zucchini and spread it into a thin layer. Continue the layering until you've run out of zucchini or space for it.
8. Sprinkle parmesan cheese on the topmost layer.
9. Cover the pan with foil and bake for 45 minutes.
10. Remove the foil and bake for 15 minutes more.
11. Allow it to cool for 15 minutes before serving. Serve immediately.
12. The lasagna will keep for 3 days in the fridge.

Nutritions: *Calories 338, Fat 34g, Carbohydrates 10g, Fiber 5g, Protein 4.7g*

Vegan Keto Scramble

Preparation:
10 Minutes

Cooking:
10-15 Minutes

Servings:
1

Ingredients

- 14 oz. firm tofu
- 3 tbsp. avocado oil
- 2 tbsp. yellow onion, diced
- 1.5 tbsp. nutritional yeast
- 1/2 tsp. turmeric
- 1/2 tsp. garlic powder
- 1/2 tsp. salt
- 1 cup baby spinach
- 3 grape tomatoes
- 3 oz. vegan cheddar cheese

Directions

1. Start by squeezing the water out of the tofu block using a clean cloth or a paper towel.
2. Grab a skillet and put it on medium heat. Sauté the chopped onion in a small amount of avocado oil until it starts to caramelize
3. Using a potato masher, crumble the tofu on the skillet. Do this thoroughly until the tofu looks a lot like scrambled eggs.
4. Drizzle some more of the avocado oil onto the mix together with the dry seasonings. Stir thoroughly and evenly distribute the flavor.
5. Cook under medium heat, occasionally stirring to avoid burning of the tofu. You'd want most of the liquid to evaporate until you get a nice chunk of scrambled tofu.
6. Fold the baby spinach, cheese, and diced tomato. Cook for a few more minutes until the cheese melted. Serve and enjoy!

Nutritions: *Calories 212, Fat 17.5g, Net Carbohydrates 4.74g, Protein 10g*

Parmesan Cheese Strips

Preparation:
30 Minutes

Cooking:
30 Minutes

Servings:
12

Directions

1. Preheat the oven to 350 degrees Fahrenheit. Prepare the baking sheet by lining it with parchment paper.
2. Form small piles of the parmesan cheese on the baking sheet. Flatten it out evenly and then sprinkle dried basil on top of the cheese.
3. Bake for 5 to 7 minutes or until you get a golden brown color with crispy edges. Take it out, serve, and enjoy!

Ingredients

- 1 cup shredded parmesan cheese
- 1 tsp. dried basil

Nutritions: *Calories 31, Fat 2g, Protein 2g*

Peanut Butter Power Granola

Preparation:
30 Minutes

Cooking:
40 Minutes

Servings:
12

Ingredients

- 1 cup shredded coconut or almond flour
- 1 1/2 cups almonds
- 1 1/2 cups pecans
- 1/3 cup swerve sweetener
- 1/3 cup vanilla whey protein powder
- 1/3 cup peanut butter
- 1/4 cup sunflower seeds
- 1/4 cup butter
- 1/4 cup water

Directions

1. Preheat the oven to 300 degrees Fahrenheit and prepare a baking sheet with parchment paper
2. Place the almonds and pecans in a food processor. Put them all in a large bowl and add the sunflower seeds, shredded coconut, vanilla, sweetener, and protein powder.
3. Melt the peanut butter and butter together in the microwave.
4. Mix the melted butter in the nut mixture and stir it thoroughly until the nuts are well-distributed.
5. Put in the water to create a lumpy mixture.
6. Scoop out small amounts of the mixture and place it on the baking sheet.
7. Bake for 30 minutes. Enjoy!

Nutritions: Calories 338k, Fat 30g, Carbohydrates 5g, Protein 9.6g, Fiber 5g

Homemade Graham Crackers

Preparation:
15 Minutes

Cooking:
1 Hour 15 Minutes

Servings:
10

Ingredients
- 1 egg, large
- 2 cups almond flour
- 1/3 cup swerve brown
- 2 tsp. cinnamon
- 1 tsp. baking powder
- 2 tbsp. melted butter
- 1 tsp. vanilla extract
- salt

Directions
1. Preheat the oven to 300 degrees Fahrenheit
2. Grab a bowl and whisk the almond flour, cinnamon, sweetener, baking powder, and salt. Stir all the ingredients together.
3. Put in the egg, molasses, melted butter, and vanilla extract. Stir until you get a dough-like consistency.
4. Roll out the dough evenly, making sure that you don't go beyond 1/4 of an inch thick. Cut the dough into the shapes you want for cooking. Transfer it to the baking tray
5. Bake for 20 to 30 minutes until it firms up. Let it cool for 30 minutes outside of the oven and then put them back in for another 30 minutes. Make sure that for the second time putting the biscuit, the temperature is not higher than 200 degrees Fahrenheit. This last step will make the biscuit crispy.

Nutritions: *Calories 156k, Fat 13.35g, Carbohydrates 6.21g, Protein 5.21g, Fiber 2.68g*

Keto No-Bake Cookies

Preparation:
15 Minutes

Cooking:
10 Minutes

Servings:
18 Cookies

Directions

1. Melt the butter in the microwave.
2. Take it out and put it in the peanut butter. Stir thoroughly.
3. Add the sweetener and coconut. Mix.
4. Spoon it onto a pan lined with parchment paper
5. Freeze for 10 minutes
6. Cut into preferred slices. Store in an airtight container in the fridge and enjoy whenever.

Ingredients

- 2/3 cup of all-natural peanut butter
- 1 cup of all-natural shredded coconut, unsweetened
- 2 tbsp. real butter
- 4 drops of vanilla lakanto

Nutritions: *80 calories*

Swiss Cheese Crunchy Nachos

Preparation:
30 Minutes

Cooking:
20 Minutes

Servings:
2

Ingredients
- 1/2 cup shredded Swiss cheese
- 1/2 cup shredded cheddar cheese
- 1/8 cup cooked bacon pieces

Directions
1. Preheat the oven to 300 degrees Fahrenheit and prepare the baking sheet by lining it with parchment paper.
2. Start by spreading the Swiss cheese on the parchment. Sprinkle it with bacon and then top it off again with the cheese.
3. Bake until the cheese has melted. This should take around 10 minutes or less.
4. Allow the cheese to cool before cutting them into triangle strips.
5. Grab another baking sheet and place the triangle cheese strips on top. Broil them for 2 to 3 minutes so they'll get chunky.

Nutritions: 280 calories per serving, 21.8 fats, 18.6g protein, 2.44g net carbohydrates

Healthy Keto Green Smoothie

Preparation:
5 Minutes

Cooking:
0 Minutes

Servings:
1

Directions

1. In a blender, combine all ingredients; blend until very smooth. Enjoy!

Ingredients

- 1/2 cup coconut milk
- 1/2 cup chopped spinach
- 1/2 medium avocado, diced
- 1 tbsp. extra virgin coconut oil
- 1/2 tsp. vanilla powder
- 1/2 cup water
- Handful of ice cubes
- 1/4 cup chocolate whey protein
- 1 tsp. matcha powder
- 5 drops liquid stevia

Nutritions: Calories: 468; Total Fat: 48.3 g; Carbs: 6 g; Dietary Fiber: 4.5 g; Sugars: 1.2 g; Protein: 14.2 g; Cholesterol: 0 mg; Sodium: 109 mg

Healthy Zucchini & Beef Frittata

Preparation:
15 Minutes

Cooking:
20 Minutes

Servings:
4

Directions

1. Preheat oven to 350°F.
2. Sauté red onion in an oven-safe skillet with butter for about 3 minutes or until tender;
3. Add garlic, beef, and zucchini and cook for about 7 minutes or until zucchini are tender and beef is cooked through.
4. Season with salt and pepper and remove from heat; cover the zucchini mixture with egg and bake for about 10 minutes or until the egg is set.
5. Serve warm.

Ingredients

- 1 tablespoon butter
- 1/2 red onion, minced
- 1 clove garlic, minced
- 8 ounce ground beef, crumbled
- 4 zucchini, thinly sliced
- 6 free-range eggs
- Pinch of sea salt
- Pinch of pepper

Nutritions: *Calories: 263; Total Fat: 13.3 g; Carbs: 8.6 g; Dietary Fiber: 2.5 g; Sugars: 4.5 g; Protein: 28.1 g; Cholesterol: 304 mg; Sodium: 229 mg*

Almond-Strawberry Smoothie

Preparation:
10 Minutes

Cooking:
0 Minutes

Servings:
2-3

Ingredients
- 500ml almond milk, unsweetened
- 1/4 cup frozen strawberries, unsweetened
- 1 scoop vegetarian protein powder
- 100ml heavy cream
- Stevia, to taste

Directions
1. Combine all the ingredients in a blender and process until smooth.
2. Serve immediately.

Nutritions: Calories: 304; Total Fat: 25 g; Carbs: 7 g; Dietary Fiber: 2.5 g; Sugars: 3.9 g; Protein: 15 g; Cholesterol: 71 mg; Sodium: 107 mg

Grilled Chicken & Avocado Power Salad with Lemon Tahini Dressing

Preparation:
10 Minutes

Cooking:
10 Minutes

Servings:
6

Ingredients

Salad
- 6 (150g) skinless boneless chicken breasts
- 2 tablespoons olive oil
- 1 tablespoon fresh lemon juice
- 1/2 teaspoon sea salt
- 1/2 teaspoon black pepper
- 6 cups mixed salad greens
- 6 hardboiled eggs
- 1 avocado
- 1/2 cup toasted chopped almonds
- 1/2 cup toasted coconut flakes
- Dressing
- 1/4 avocado
- 2 tablespoons salted tahini
- 2 tablespoons extra virgin olive oil
- 2 tablespoons fresh lemon juice

Directions

1. In a small bowl, mix 1 tablespoon of fresh lemon juice, olive oil, sea salt, and pepper; rub over the chicken and grill on medium-high heat for about 5 minutes per side or until cooked through and golden brown on the outside; remove from heat and let cool before slicing.
2. In a blender, combine together the remaining olive oil, fresh lemon juice, avocado, and tahini; blend until very smooth.
3. In a serving bowl, combine mixed green salad, diced boiled egg, avocado, and toasted almonds and coconut flakes. Pour in the dressing and toss to combine well. Enjoy!

Nutritions: *Calories: 452; Total Fat: 31.9 g; Carbs: 9.7 g; Dietary Fiber: 4.9 g; Sugar: 1.5 g; Protein: 33.9 g; Cholesterol: 226 mg; Sodium: 288 mg*

Pan-Seared Salmon with Crunchy Cabbage Slaw & Toasted Macadamias

Preparation: 15 Minutes

Cooking: 10 Minutes

Servings: 8

Ingredients

- 4 x 180g salmon skin-on
- 1 1/2 tablespoons olive oil
- 4 cups thinly sliced cabbage
- 2 teaspoons raw honey
- 1/4 cup fresh lime juice
- 2 spring onions, chopped
- 1 yellow capsicum, thinly sliced
- 200g seedless white grapes, halved
- 1/2 cup fresh mint leaves
- 1/2 cup fresh coriander leaves
- 1/2 cup chopped toasted macadamias
- Lime wedges

Directions

1. Heat half tablespoon of oil in a skillet over medium heat; place in salmon, skin side down and cook for about 5 minutes or until the skin is crisp; turn over to cook the other side for about 3 minutes or until cooked through.
2. In the meantime, whisk together raw honey, lime juice, lime zest, salt, and the remaining oil until well blended; add in grapes, cabbage, spring onions, capsicum, mint, and coriander. Stir in salt and pepper.
3. Divide the cabbage slaw among serving plates and top each serving with salmon. Sprinkle with toasted macadamia and garnish with lime wedges. Enjoy!

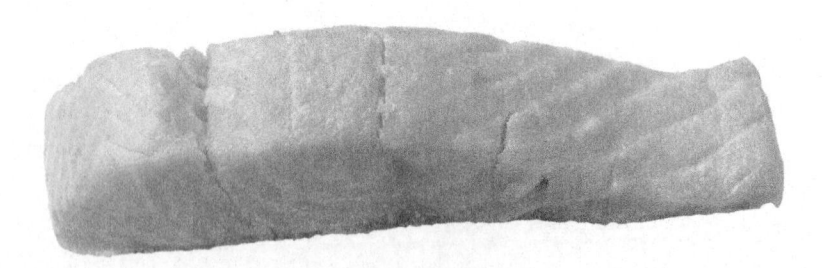

Nutritions: *Calories: 638; Total Fat: 45 g; Carbs: 15 g; Dietary Fiber: 5 g; Sugars: 11 g; Protein: 43 g; Cholesterol: 112 mg; Sodium: 215 mg*

Sautéed Scallops with Spinach & Mushrooms Sauce

Preparation:
10 Minutes

Cooking:
5 Minutes

Servings:
8

Ingredients

- 24 shelled and cleaned scallops
- 3 tbsp. groundnut oil
- 2 cups spinach
- 2 cups mushrooms, sliced
- 4 tbsp. butter
- nutmeg, grated

Directions

1. Melt half of the butter in a saucepan until sizzling; stir in mushrooms for about 1 minute, and then stir in spinach. Cook for about 1 minute or until wilted. Drain spinach and mushrooms in a colander over a bowl. Keep warm.
2. In a separate pan, heat oil until hot, but not smoking; add scallops and sauté for about 3 minutes without disturbing them. Add a knob of butter and then turn the scallops. Season with salt and pepper and then baste with melted butter. Continue cooking for 5 minutes more or until scallops are ready.
3. Meanwhile, return reserved spinach-mushroom juices to the pan they were cooked in and add the remaining butter; season the sauce with nutmeg, salt, and pepper.
4. Arrange mushrooms and spinach on serving platters and sit scallops on top. Spoon the butter sauce around and serve.

Nutritions: *Calories: 229; Total Fat: 16.9 g; Carbs: 3.1 g; Dietary fiber: 0.4 g; Sugars: 0.4 g; Protein: 15.9 g; Cholesterol: 45 mg; Sodium: 193 mg*

Chicken and Buckwheat Salad Served with Chili-Tomato Salsa

Preparation:
20 Minutes

Cooking:
20 Minutes

Servings:
1

Ingredients

- 1 cup fresh lemon juice
- 2 teaspoons ground turmeric
- 2 tablespoons extra-virgin olive oil
- 4 (100g each) chicken breasts, skinless, boneless
- 1 cup chopped kale
- 1 teaspoon chopped ginger
- 1 large red onion, sliced
- 1 cup buckwheat
- For the salsa
- 1 large tomato, finely chopped
- 1 tablespoon capers, finely chopped
- 1 bird's eye chili, finely chopped
- Juice of 1/4 lemon
- 1/2 cup parsley, finely chopped

Directions

1. Make the salsa: mix chopped tomato, capers, chili, lemon juice, and parsley in a large bowl.
2. Preheat your oven to 450°F.
3. In a large bowl, mix lemon juice, 1 teaspoon turmeric, and a splash of extra virgin olive oil; add the chicken and stir to combine well. Marinate for about 10 minutes.
4. Set an ovenproof pan over medium heat and add the chicken; cook for about 4 minutes per side or until lightly browned. Transfer to the preheated oven and bake for about 10 minutes remove from the oven and
5. Remove the chicken from the oven and keep warm.
6. In the meantime, steam kale in a steamer for about 5 minutes.
7. Fry ginger and red onion in a splash of extra virgin olive oil until tender; stir in kale and cook for about 1 minute.
8. Follow package instructions to cook buckwheat with the remaining turmeric.
9. Serve the buckwheat with chicken, veggies, and salsa.

Nutritions: Calories: 335; Total Fat: 11.6g; Carbs: 2.6g; Dietary Fiber: 4.3g; sugars: 5.8g; Protein: 22.5g; Cholesterol: 51mg; Sodium: 224mg

Avocado, Fennel & Heirloom Tomato Salad

Preparation:
10 Minutes

Cooking:
0 Minutes

Servings:
4

Ingredients

- 1 large avocado, sliced
- 1 red onion, thinly sliced
- 1 large fennel bulb, chopped
- 4 medium tomatoes, chopped
- 1 tablespoon avocado oil
- 3 tablespoons extra virgin olive oil
- 2 tablespoons fresh lime juice
- 2 tablespoons chopped fresh cilantro
- 1/8 teaspoon chili powder
- 1/8 teaspoon smoked paprika
- 1/8 teaspoon sea salt

Directions

1. In a bowl, combine avocado, red onion, fennel, and tomatoes.
2. In a small bowl, whisk together avocado oil, extra virgin olive oil, lime juice, cilantro, chili powder paprika, and salt; pour over the avocado mixture and toss to combine well. Enjoy!

Nutritions: *Calories: 231; Total Fat: 21 g; Carbs: 12 g; Dietary Fiber: 5.7 g; Sugars: 4.7 g; Protein: 2.4 g; Cholesterol: 0 mg; Sodium: 70 mg*

Spiced Turkey Served with Avocado Relish

Preparation:
10 Minutes

Cooking:
5 Minutes

Servings:
2

Ingredients

- 225g turkey cutlets
- 1/2 tsp. 5-spice powder
- 2 tbsp. extra virgin olive oil
- 1 tbsp. chili powder
- A good pinch kosher salt
-
- For the avocado relish:
- 1/2 avocado, diced 1 seedless grapefruit, cut into segments and discarding the membranes
- 1 small Vidalia onion, minced
- 1 tsp. red wine vinegar
- 1 tbsp. fresh cilantro, chopped
- 1 tsp. natural honey

Directions

1. Combine the avocado, grapefruit segments, onion, honey, vinegar, and cilantro and toss well to combine.
2. Next, combine all the spices for the turkey in a shallow bowl then dredge the cutlets in the spice mix.
3. Add the oil to a pan over medium heat and sear the turkey until cooked to desired doneness for about 3-5 minutes on each side.
4. Serve hot with the relish.
5. Enjoy!

Nutritions: Calories: 440; Total Fat: 30.1 g; Carbs: 9.7 g; Dietary Fiber: 5.4 g; Sugars: 2 g; Protein: 34.8 g; Cholesterol: 85 mg; Sodium: 121 mg

Satisfying Parmesan Stuffed Tomatoes

Preparation:
10 Minutes

Cooking:
10 Minutes

Servings:
3

Directions

1. Preheat your oven to 400 degrees.
2. Arrange the halved tomatoes on a baking sheet and stuff each half with minced garlic and parmesan cheese. Sprinkle each with Italian seasoning, salt, and pepper.
3. Drizzle with olive oil and bake in the oven for about 10 minutes or until cheese is bubbly. Serve warm topped with chopped parsley. Enjoy!

Ingredients

- 3 large tomatoes, halved
- 1/2 cup Parmesan cheese, grated
- 2 cloves garlic, minced
- 1 tablespoon Italian seasoning
- 1/8 teaspoon sea salt
- 1/8 teaspoon pepper
- 2 tablespoons olive oil
- Chopped parsley

Nutritions: *Calories: 257; Total Fat: 19.3 g; Carbs: 10.9 g; Dietary fiber: 2.5 g; Sugars: 5.4 g; Protein: 14.4 g; Cholesterol: 30 mg; Sodium: 447 mg*

Healthy Garlic Creamed Sautéed Spinach

Preparation:
5 Minutes

Cooking:
5 Minutes

Servings:
2

Directions

1. Melt butter in a skillet and sauté garlic until fragrant. Stir in spinach, lemon juice, and coconut cream and cook for about 3 minutes.
2. Stir in salt and pepper and remove from heat.
3. Serve spinach garnished with lemon wedges.

Ingredients

- 2 tablespoons melted butter
- 4 cloves garlic, thinly sliced
- 2 cups fresh spinach, rinsed
- 1/4 cup coconut cream
- 1 teaspoon lemon juice
- Sea salt & pepper

Nutritions: Calories: 187; Total Fat: 18.8 g; Carbs: 4.8 g; Dietary fiber: 1.5 g; Sugars: 1.3 g; Protein: 2.1 g; Cholesterol: 31 mg; Sodium: 112 mg

CHAPTER 12.
Brochure Associated with The Book

My food diary (40 days of KETO diet & intermittent fasting) Daily planner to keep track of food, physical activity, and much more to get back in shape in 40 days while staying motivated

MY PERSONAL DATA	
SURNAME	
FIRST NAME	
DATE OF BIRTH	
HEIGHT	
WEIGHT ON DAY 1	
WEIGHT ON DAY 40	
SMOKER	NON SMOKER
DISEASES / INTOLERANCES / ALLERGIES	
TARGET: BE IN GOOD HEALTH SLIMMING MUSCLE DEVELOPMENT GAIN WEIGHT	

Day 1

Place where the meal was eaten	Mood	Drinks	If we got up from the table full / too full/hungry	Any swelling/discomfort in digestion	
					Breakfast
					Mid-morning Snack
					Lunch
					Afternoon Snack
					Dinner
Intestinal health (number of bowel movements, shape, color, consistency of stools)					
Whether we played sports (what kind of sport, for how long)					

Day 2

Place where the meal was eaten	Mood	Drinks	If we got up from the table full / too full/hungry	Any swelling/discomfort in digestion	
					Breakfast
					Mid-morning Snack
					Lunch
					Afternoon Snack
					Dinner
Intestinal health (number of bowel movements, shape, color, consistency of stools)						
Whether we played sports (what kind of sport, for how long)						

Day 3

Place where the meal was eaten	Mood	Drinks	If we got up from the table full / too full/hungry	Any swelling/discomfort in digestion	
					Breakfast
					Mid-morning Snack
					Lunch
					Afternoon Snack
					Dinner
Intestinal health (number of bowel movements, shape, color, consistency of stools)						
Whether we played sports (what kind of sport, for how long)						

Day 4

Place where the meal was eaten	Mood	Drinks	If we got up from the table full / too full/hungry	Any swelling/discomfort in digestion	
					Breakfast
					Mid-morning Snack
					Lunch
					Afternoon Snack
					Dinner
Intestinal health (number of bowel movements, shape, color, consistency of stools)					
Whether we played sports (what kind of sport, for how long)					

Day 5

Place where the meal was eaten	Mood	Drinks	If we got up from the table full / too full/hungry	Any swelling/discomfort in digestion	
					Breakfast
					Mid-morning Snack
					Lunch
					Afternoon Snack
					Dinner
Intestinal health (number of bowel movements, shape, color, consistency of stools)					
Whether we played sports (what kind of sport, for how long)					

Day 6

Place where the meal was eaten	Mood	Drinks	If we got up from the table full / too full/hungry	Any swelling/discomfort in digestion	
					Breakfast
					Mid-morning Snack
					Lunch
					Afternoon Snack
					Dinner

Intestinal health (number of bowel movements, shape, color, consistency of stools)

Whether we played sports (what kind of sport, for how long)

Day 7

Place where the meal was eaten	Mood	Drinks	If we got up from the table full / too full/hungry	Any swelling/discomfort in digestion	
					Breakfast
					Mid-morning Snack
					Lunch
					Afternoon Snack
					Dinner
Intestinal health (number of bowel movements, shape, color, consistency of stools)					
Whether we played sports (what kind of sport, for how long)					

Day 8

Place where the meal was eaten	Mood	Drinks	If we got up from the table full / too full/hungry	Any swelling/discomfort in digestion	
					Breakfast
					Mid-morning Snack
					Lunch
					Afternoon Snack
					Dinner
Intestinal health (number of bowel movements, shape, color, consistency of stools)					
Whether we played sports (what kind of sport, for how long)					

Day 9

Place where the meal was eaten	Mood	Drinks	If we got up from the table full / too full/hungry	Any swelling/discomfort in digestion	
					Breakfast
					Mid-morning Snack
					Lunch
					Afternoon Snack
					Dinner
Intestinal health (number of bowel movements, shape, color, consistency of stools)					
Whether we played sports (what kind of sport, for how long)					

Day 10

Place where the meal was eaten	Mood	Drinks	If we got up from the table full / too full/hungry	Any swelling/discomfort in digestion	
					Breakfast
					Mid-morning Snack
					Lunch
					Afternoon Snack
					Dinner
Intestinal health (number of bowel movements, shape, color, consistency of stools)					
Whether we played sports (what kind of sport, for how long)					

Day 11

Place where the meal was eaten	Mood	Drinks	If we got up from the table full / too full/hungry	Any swelling/discomfort in digestion	
					Breakfast
					Mid-morning Snack
					Lunch
					Afternoon Snack
					Dinner
Intestinal health (number of bowel movements, shape, color, consistency of stools)					
Whether we played sports (what kind of sport, for how long)					

Day 12

Place where the meal was eaten	Mood	Drinks	If we got up from the table full / too full/hungry	Any swelling/discomfort in digestion	
					Breakfast
					Mid-morning Snack
					Lunch
					Afternoon Snack
					Dinner
Intestinal health (number of bowel movements, shape, color, consistency of stools)					
Whether we played sports (what kind of sport, for how long)					

Day 13

Place where the meal was eaten	Mood	Drinks	If we got up from the table full / too full/hungry	Any swelling/discomfort in digestion	
					Breakfast
					Mid-morning Snack
					Lunch
					Afternoon Snack
					Dinner
Intestinal health (number of bowel movements, shape, color, consistency of stools)					
Whether we played sports (what kind of sport, for how long)					

Day 14

Place where the meal was eaten	Mood	Drinks	If we got up from the table full / too full/hungry	Any swelling/discomfort in digestion	
					Breakfast
					Mid-morning Snack
					Lunch
					Afternoon Snack
					Dinner
Intestinal health (number of bowel movements, shape, color, consistency of stools)					
Whether we played sports (what kind of sport, for how long)					

Day 15

Place where the meal was eaten	Mood	Drinks	If we got up from the table full / too full/hungry	Any swelling/discomfort in digestion	
					Breakfast
					Mid-morning Snack
					Lunch
					Afternoon Snack
					Dinner
Intestinal health (number of bowel movements, shape, color, consistency of stools)					
Whether we played sports (what kind of sport, for how long)					

Day 16

Place where the meal was eaten	Mood	Drinks	If we got up from the table full / too full/hungry	Any swelling/discomfort in digestion	
					Breakfast
					Mid-morning Snack
					Lunch
					Afternoon Snack
					Dinner
Intestinal health (number of bowel movements, shape, color, consistency of stools)					
Whether we played sports (what kind of sport, for how long)					

Day 17

Place where the meal was eaten	Mood	Drinks	If we got up from the table full / too full/hungry	Any swelling/discomfort in digestion	
					Breakfast
					Mid-morning Snack
					Lunch
					Afternoon Snack
					Dinner
Intestinal health (number of bowel movements, shape, color, consistency of stools)					
Whether we played sports (what kind of sport, for how long)					

Day 18

Place where the meal was eaten	Mood	Drinks	If we got up from the table full / too full/hungry	Any swelling/discomfort in digestion	
					Breakfast
					Mid-morning Snack
					Lunch
					Afternoon Snack
					Dinner
Intestinal health (number of bowel movements, shape, color, consistency of stools)					
Whether we played sports (what kind of sport, for how long)					

Day 19

Place where the meal was eaten	Mood	Drinks	If we got up from the table full / too full/hungry	Any swelling/discomfort in digestion	
					Breakfast
					Mid-morning Snack
					Lunch
					Afternoon Snack
					Dinner
Intestinal health (number of bowel movements, shape, color, consistency of stools)					
Whether we played sports (what kind of sport, for how long)					

Day 20

Place where the meal was eaten	Mood	Drinks	If we got up from the table full / too full/hungry	Any swelling/discomfort in digestion	
					Breakfast
					Mid-morning Snack
					Lunch
					Afternoon Snack
					Dinner

Intestinal health (number of bowel movements, shape, color, consistency of stools)

Whether we played sports (what kind of sport, for how long)

Day 21

Place where the meal was eaten	Mood	Drinks	If we got up from the table full / too full/hungry	Any swelling/discomfort in digestion	
					Breakfast
					Mid-morning Snack
					Lunch
					Afternoon Snack
					Dinner

Intestinal health (number of bowel movements, shape, color, consistency of stools)

Whether we played sports (what kind of sport, for how long)

Day 22

Place where the meal was eaten	Mood	Drinks	If we got up from the table full / too full/hungry	Any swelling/discomfort in digestion	
					Breakfast
					Mid-morning Snack
					Lunch
					Afternoon Snack
					Dinner

Intestinal health (number of bowel movements, shape, color, consistency of stools)

Whether we played sports (what kind of sport, for how long)

Day 23

Place where the meal was eaten	Mood	Drinks	If we got up from the table full / too full/hungry	Any swelling/discomfort in digestion	
					Breakfast
					Mid-morning Snack
					Lunch
					Afternoon Snack
					Dinner
Intestinal health (number of bowel movements, shape, color, consistency of stools)					
Whether we played sports (what kind of sport, for how long)					

Day 24

Place where the meal was eaten	Mood	Drinks	If we got up from the table full / too full/hungry	Any swelling/discomfort in digestion	
					Breakfast
					Mid-morning Snack
					Lunch
					Afternoon Snack
					Dinner

Intestinal health (number of bowel movements, shape, color, consistency of stools)

Whether we played sports (what kind of sport, for how long)

Day 25

Place where the meal was eaten	Mood	Drinks	If we got up from the table full / too full/hungry	Any swelling/discomfort in digestion	
					Breakfast
					Mid-morning Snack
					Lunch
					Afternoon Snack
					Dinner
Intestinal health (number of bowel movements, shape, color, consistency of stools)					
Whether we played sports (what kind of sport, for how long)					

Day 26

Place where the meal was eaten	Mood	Drinks	If we got up from the table full / too full/hungry	Any swelling/discomfort in digestion	
					Breakfast
					Mid-morning Snack
					Lunch
					Afternoon Snack
					Dinner
Intestinal health (number of bowel movements, shape, color, consistency of stools)					
Whether we played sports (what kind of sport, for how long)					

Day 27

Place where the meal was eaten	Mood	Drinks	If we got up from the table full / too full/hungry	Any swelling/discomfort in digestion	
					Breakfast
					Mid-morning Snack
					Lunch
					Afternoon Snack
					Dinner
Intestinal health (number of bowel movements, shape, color, consistency of stools)					
Whether we played sports (what kind of sport, for how long)					

Day 28

Place where the meal was eaten	Mood	Drinks	If we got up from the table full / too full/hungry	Any swelling/discomfort in digestion	
					Breakfast
					Mid-morning Snack
					Lunch
					Afternoon Snack
					Dinner
Intestinal health (number of bowel movements, shape, color, consistency of stools)					
Whether we played sports (what kind of sport, for how long)					

Day 29

Place where the meal was eaten	Mood	Drinks	If we got up from the table full / too full/hungry	Any swelling/discomfort in digestion	
					Breakfast
					Mid-morning Snack
					Lunch
					Afternoon Snack
					Dinner
Intestinal health (number of bowel movements, shape, color, consistency of stools)					
Whether we played sports (what kind of sport, for how long)					

Day 30

Place where the meal was eaten	Mood	Drinks	If we got up from the table full / too full/hungry	Any swelling/discomfort in digestion	
					Breakfast
					Mid-morning Snack
					Lunch
					Afternoon Snack
					Dinner

Intestinal health (number of bowel movements, shape, color, consistency of stools)

Whether we played sports (what kind of sport, for how long)

Day 31

Place where the meal was eaten	Mood	Drinks	If we got up from the table full / too full/hungry	Any swelling/discomfort in digestion	
					Breakfast
					Mid-morning Snack
					Lunch
					Afternoon Snack
					Dinner
Intestinal health (number of bowel movements, shape, color, consistency of stools)						
Whether we played sports (what kind of sport, for how long)						

Day 32

Place where the meal was eaten	Mood	Drinks	If we got up from the table full / too full/hungry	Any swelling/discomfort in digestion	
					Breakfast
					Mid-morning Snack
					Lunch
					Afternoon Snack
					Dinner

Intestinal health (number of bowel movements, shape, color, consistency of stools)

Whether we played sports (what kind of sport, for how long)

Day 33

Place where the meal was eaten	Mood	Drinks	If we got up from the table full / too full/hungry	Any swelling/discomfort in digestion	
					Breakfast
					Mid-morning Snack
					Lunch
					Afternoon Snack
					Dinner
Intestinal health (number of bowel movements, shape, color, consistency of stools)					
Whether we played sports (what kind of sport, for how long)					

Day 34

Place where the meal was eaten	Mood	Drinks	If we got up from the table full / too full/hungry	Any swelling/discomfort in digestion	
					Breakfast
					Mid-morning Snack
					Lunch
					Afternoon Snack
					Dinner

Intestinal health (number of bowel movements, shape, color, consistency of stools)

Whether we played sports (what kind of sport, for how long)

Day 35

Place where the meal was eaten	Mood	Drinks	If we got up from the table full / too full/hungry	Any swelling/discomfort in digestion	
					Breakfast
					Mid-morning Snack
					Lunch
					Afternoon Snack
					Dinner
Intestinal health (number of bowel movements, shape, color, consistency of stools)					
Whether we played sports (what kind of sport, for how long)					

Day 36

Place where the meal was eaten	Mood	Drinks	If we got up from the table full / too full/hungry	Any swelling/discomfort in digestion	
					Breakfast
					Mid-morning Snack
					Lunch
					Afternoon Snack
					Dinner

Intestinal health (number of bowel movements, shape, color, consistency of stools)

Whether we played sports (what kind of sport, for how long)

Day 37

Place where the meal was eaten	Mood	Drinks	If we got up from the table full / too full/hungry	Any swelling/discomfort in digestion	
					Breakfast
					Mid-morning Snack
					Lunch
					Afternoon Snack
					Dinner
Intestinal health (number of bowel movements, shape, color, consistency of stools)					
Whether we played sports (what kind of sport, for how long)					

Day 38

Place where the meal was eaten	Mood	Drinks	If we got up from the table full / too full/hungry	Any swelling/discomfort in digestion	
					Breakfast
					Mid-morning Snack
					Lunch
					Afternoon Snack
					Dinner
Intestinal health (number of bowel movements, shape, color, consistency of stools)						
Whether we played sports (what kind of sport, for how long)						

Day 39

Place where the meal was eaten	Mood	Drinks	If we got up from the table full / too full/hungry	Any swelling/discomfort in digestion	
					Breakfast
					Mid-morning Snack
					Lunch
					Afternoon Snack
					Dinner
Intestinal health (number of bowel movements, shape, color, consistency of stools)					
Whether we played sports (what kind of sport, for how long)					

Day 40

Place where the meal was eaten	Mood	Drinks	If we got up from the table full / too full/hungry	Any swelling/discomfort in digestion	
					Breakfast
					Mid-morning Snack
					Lunch
					Afternoon Snack
					Dinner
Intestinal health (number of bowel movements, shape, color, consistency of stools)					
Whether we played sports (what kind of sport, for how long)					

Conclusion

I hope it was informative and provided you with tons of useful information to help change the rest of your life through each segment of your journey by providing you with the fundamentals of the ketogenic way of living. Each tasty recipe is designed to keep you in ketosis. The first few weeks may be a little stressful but hang in there because it will become easier.

While the science still argues about it to this day, it seems more logical that breakfast is the most important meal of the day considering that you would not have eaten for the past 8 hours whereas the interval between breakfast and lunch, and lunch and dinner is 5 or 6 hours at best. Dinner should be small because your body does not need to expend that much energy when you are sleeping anyway. So the excess energy becomes fat.

So keep dinner light. For one, it helps you lose weight. Another reason is if you have a heavy dinner, your body will strain itself trying to digest everything. That means your body would remain active until all the food is digested, meaning that you will not get restful sleep if you can sleep at all.

Bottom line: Eat light and eat dinner at least 4 hours before bedtime. Any sooner and you will have a hard time sleeping.

Once you have all of the chief spices and other fixings stocked in your Keto kitchen, the shopping list for the following week will be much easier. As a quick reminder, keep these simple tips in mind as you go through your ketogenic journey:

- Drink plenty of water daily and limit the intake of sugar-sweetened beverages.
- It is essential to attempt to use only half of your typical serving of salad dressing or butter.
- Use only fat-free or low-fat condiments.
- Add a serving of vegetables to your dinner and lunch menus.
- Add a serving of fruit as a snack or enjoy your meal. The skin also contains additional nutrients. Dried and canned fruits are quick and easy to use. However, make sure they don't have added sugar.
- Read the food labels and make choices that keep you in line with ketosis.

- For a snack, have some frozen yogurt (fat-free or low-fat), nuts or unsalted pretzels, raw veggies, or unsalted popcorn.
- Prepare cut veggies such as bell pepper strips, mixed greens, and carrots. Store them in small baggies for a quick on-the-go healthy choice.

One of the easiest ways to stay on your plan is to remove the temptations. Remove the chocolate, candy, bread, pasta, rice, and sugary sodas you have supplied in your kitchen. If you live alone, this is an easy task. It is a bit more challenging if you have a family. The diet will also be useful for them if you plan your meals using the recipes included in this book.

If you cheat, that has to count also. It will be a reminder of your indulgence, but it will help keep you in line. Others may believe you are obsessed with the plan, but it is your health and wellbeing that you are improving.

When you go shopping for your ketogenic essentials be sure you take your new skills, a grocery list, and search the labels. Almost every food item in today's grocery store has a nutrition label. Be sure you read each of the ingredients to discover any hiding carbs to keep your ketosis in line. You will be glad you took the extra time.

Best of Luck!

Printed in Great Britain
by Amazon